The power of citizens and professionals in welfare encounters

MANCHESTER
1824

Manchester University Press

SOCIAL AND POLITICAL POWER

Series editor: Mark Haugaard

Power is one of the most fundamental concepts in social science. Yet, despite the undisputed centrality of power to social and political life, few have agreed on exactly what it is or how it manifests itself. *Social and Political Power* is a book series which provides a forum for this absolutely central, and much debated, social phenomenon. The series is theoretical, in both a social scientific and normative sense, yet also empirical in its orientation. Theoretically it is oriented towards the Anglo-American tradition, including Dahl and Lukes, as well as to the Continental perspectives, influenced either by Foucault and Bourdieu, or by Arendt and the Frankfurt School. Empirically, the series provides an intellectual forum for power research from the disciplines of sociology, political science and the other social sciences, and also for policy-oriented analysis.

Already published

Power, luck and freedom: Collected essays
Keith Dowding

Neoliberal power and public management reforms
Peter Triantafillou

Evaluating parental power: An exercise in pluralist political theory
Allyn Fives

The power of citizens and professionals in welfare encounters

The influence of bureaucracy, market and psychology

Nanna Mik-Meyer

Manchester University Press

Published by Manchester University Press
Oxford Road, Manchester M13 9PL

www.manchesteruniversitypress.co.uk

British Library Cataloguing-in-Publication Data
A catalogue record for this book is available from the British Library

Library of Congress Cataloging-in-Publication Data applied for

ISBN   978 1 5261 1028 2   hardback
ISBN   978 1 5261 1029 9   paperback

First published 2017
Paperback published 2022

Typeset by
Deanta Global Publishing Services, Chennai, India

Contents

Contents

Series editor's introduction

Bertrand Russell once argued that power is to social science what energy is to physics (Russell 1938: 10). While power is one of the most important concepts in the social sciences, it is also one of the most complex and elusive to research.

Weber's analysis of power and authority (1947, 1978) is one of the first social scientific discussions of power, and it influenced the US power debates, which developed post–World War Two. In these debates, Dahl's careful analysis stands out for its clarity in providing us with a conceptual vocabulary of power (Dahl 1957, 1968). This includes an agency-based, exercise and decision-making definition of power; conceptualized in terms of powerful actors (A) making subordinates (B) do something that they would not otherwise do. This exercise of power is distinct from resources (that may or may not be exercised), and it provides power-holders with power of specific scope. However, while providing a new set of conceptual tools to analyse about power relations, Dahl's work was subject to sustained critique from Bachrach and Baratz and others, who argued that power is also exercised through structural biases that are not necessarily reducible to overt decision-making (Bachrach and Baratz 1962). Lukes followed this critique with his theorization of the third dimension of power (Lukes 1974), which concerns the mobilization of belief and ideology to legitimise power relations of domination. The three-dimensional model was applied in a richly textured empirical study of Appalachian mining communities (Gaventa 1982). Overall, as the three-dimensional power debates develop, the focus shifts from actions of the dominating actor A to the counterintuitive and fascinating phenomenon that subordinate actors B often appear to actively acquiesce or participate in their own domination.

In a qualified critique of Lukes, Scott argued that appearances are often deceptive (Scott 1990). The relationship between public and private discourse renders the working of three-dimensional power more complex than any simplistic images of the oppressed willingly participating in their own domination, or internalizing false consciousness. In turn, Scott's work has inspired an ongoing power literature on the complexities of resistance versus acquiescence.

In the 1980s, under the influence of the translation of Foucault's work (e.g., Foucault 1979, 1982), the Anglophone power debates shifted towards more epistemic and ontological analysis, which resonated with the shift of emphasis from the powerful to the conditions of the oppressed. This gave rise to fascinating work on the relation between power and discourse, power and truth, the way power influences the ontological formation of social subjects through discipline and how governmentality has changed systemic power relations (including Clegg 1989; Flyvbjerg 1998; Hayward 2000; Laclau 2005; Dean 2010). However, in critique, many have argued that neo-Foucauldians tend to lose sight of the significance of individual agency (Lukes 2005).

Bridging the intellectual divide between those following the Dahl–Lukes trajectory and the neo-Foucauldians, another important thread to the power debates comes from Giddens (1984) and Bourdieu's (1989) conceptualizations of structure as a verb. This way of thinking provides us with conceptual tools for making sense of how agents both structure and are structured by relations of power.

In international relations, the shift from agency towards systemic, epistemic and ontological perceptions of power took the form of a gradual move from a realist focus on resources to a more idealist emphasis upon soft power (Nye 1990, 2011). Similarly, in rational choice theory, there emerged an emphasis upon the systemic situatedness of strategic choices (Dowding 2016).

The effect of interrogating the social contexts and social ontology of agents has caused many theorists to re-evaluate the nature of power normatively, moving away from the automatic equation between power and domination to a perception of power as a condition of possibility for agency, and thus freedom (Morriss 2002, 2009). Thus, freedom and power move from being opposing categories to being mutually constitutive. Associated with this normative re-evaluation, power theorists distinguish between power-to, power-with and power-over (Allen 1998, 1999; Pansardi 2012). To begin with, power-over was considered a normative negative, suggesting oppression, while power-to and power-with were the positives. However, some theorists argue power-over can also have emancipatory, as well as the more obvious dominating, aspects (Haugaard 2012).

Within these theoretical contexts, Nanna Mik-Meyer's book, *The power of citizens and professionals in welfare encounters: The influence of bureaucracy, market and psychology*, constitutes an ethnographically rich account of the microphysics of power relations between staff and citizens in welfare organizations. The described encounters take place in bureaucratic contexts, which suggest Weberian theories of bureaucratic authority, coupled with one-dimensional, top-down, exercises of power. Alternatively, drawing upon Foucault and Bourdieu, the reader might expect 'experts versus disempowered citizens', and clear boundaries of what counts as relevant 'truth' and epistemic knowledge. However, as the book's analyses show, these professionals do not establish themselves as the undisputed holders of expertise or power-over. The citizens emerge with significant authoritative power derived from their everyday knowledge of their own experiences, and of influential systems of thought. Thus, professionals do not have a monopoly of truth. Furthermore, it is often contested which realms of knowledge are considered valid sources of epistemic cultural capital. Rather than one episteme, Mik-Meyer shows contested knowledge that includes bureaucratic criteria (as one might expect), popular psychology, market values and the everyday life of the citizen, all of which pull in different directions. This is a brilliant example of how well-grounded empirical research often confounds, or makes more complex, our theoretical models of power relations.

In general, the book series, *Social and Political Power*, seeks to build upon these rich traditions of power analysis, which currently make the study of social and political power one of the most vibrant fields in the social and political sciences. It also builds upon the success of the *Journal of Political Power*, which provides an important forum for article analysis, while this book series facilitates longer works on social and political power.

The book series is open to any of the multiplicity of traditions of power analysis, and it welcomes research that is theoretically oriented, as well as empirical research on power or practitioner-oriented applications.

Mark Haugaard,
National University of Ireland, Galway, Ireland

References

Allen, A. (1998). Rethinking power. *Hyptia*, 13(1), 21–40.
Allen, A. (1999). *The Power of Feminist Theory: Domination, Resistance, Solidarity*. Boulder: Westview Press.
Bachrach, P., and M. S. Baratz. (1962). Two faces of power. *American Political Science Review*, 56(4), 947–52.
Bourdieu, P. (1989). Social space and symbolic power. *Sociological Theory*, 7(1), 14–25.
Clegg, S. (1989). *Frameworks of Power*. London: Sage.

Dahl, R. A. (1957). The concept of power. *Behavioural Science*, *2*(3), 201–15.

Dahl, R. A. (1968). Power. In D. L. Shills (Ed.), *International Encyclopedia of the Social Sciences* (Vol. *12*, pp. 405–15). New York: Macmillan.

Dean, M. (2010). *Governmentality: Power and Rule in Modern Society* (2nd ed.). London: Sage.

Dowding, K. (2016). *Power, Luck and Freedom: Collected Essays*. Social and Political Power Series. Manchester: Manchester University Press.

Flyvbjerg, B. (1998). *Rationality and Power: Democracy in Practice*. Chicago: University of Chicago Press.

Foucault, M. (1979). *Discipline and Punish: The Birth of the Prison*. Harmondsworth: Penguin.

Foucault, M. (1982). The subject and power. In H. L. Dreyfus and P. Rabinow (Eds.), *Michel Foucault: Beyond Structuralism and Hermeneutics* (pp. 208–26). London: Harvester Wheatsheaf.

Gaventa, J. (1982). *Power and Powerlessness: Quiescence and Rebellion in an Appalachian Valley*. Oxford: Clarendon Press.

Giddens, A. (1984). *The Constitution of Society*. Cambridge: Polity Press.

Haugaard, M. (2012). Rethinking the four dimensions of power. *Journal of Political Power*, 5(1), 35–54.

Hayward, C. (2000). *De-Facing Power*. Cambridge: Cambridge University Press.

Laclau, E. (2005). *On Populist Reason*. London: Verso.

Lukes, S. (1974). *Power: A Radical View*. London: Macmillan.

Lukes, S. (2005). *Power: A Radical View* (2nd ed.). Basingstoke: Palgrave Macmillan.

Morriss, P. (2002). *Power: A Philosophical Analysis* (2nd ed.). Manchester: Manchester University Press.

Morriss, P. (2009). Power and liberalism. In S. Clegg and M. Haugaard (Eds.), *The Sage Handbook of Power* (pp. 54–70). London: Sage.

Nye, J. S. (1990). Soft power. *Foreign Policy*, *80*, 153–72.

Nye, J. S. (2011). Power and foreign policy. *Journal of Political Power*, 4(1), 9–24.

Pansardi, P. (2012). Power to and power over: Two distinct concepts? *Journal of Political Power*, 5(1), 73–89.

Russell, B. (1938). *Power: A New Social Analysis*. London: George Allen & Unwin.

Scott, J. C. (1990). *Domination and the Arts of Resistance: Hidden Transcripts*. New Haven: Yale University Press.

Weber, M. (1947). *The Theory of Social and Economic Organization* (T. Parsons, Ed.). New York: Free Press.

Weber, M. (1978). *Economy and Society: An Outline of Interpretive Sociology* (G. Roth and C. Wittich, Eds., 2 vols.). Berkeley: University of California Press.

Preface

Ever since I did my first six months of fieldwork as a graduate student in an activation programme for unemployed citizens (Mik-Meyer 1999), I have been quite puzzled by the progression of the encounter between citizens and welfare workers. This puzzlement has been further strengthened by my subsequent doctoral research project on rehabilitation work (Mik-Meyer 2004), my post doc research on the situations of overweight people (Mik-Meyer 2010b, 2014, 2015b) and recent projects on functional disorders (Mik-Meyer and Johansen 2009; Mik-Meyer 2010a, 2011; Mik-Meyer and Obling 2012) and disability, marginalisation and work (Mik-Meyer 2015a, 2016a, 2016b, 2016c). What has puzzled me the most is the often contradictory norms of what welfare work is (or ought to be) when observing and interviewing citizens and the staff whom they encounter. I have found simultaneous and overlapping expectations of standardised documentation, emphasis on legislation as well as co-production, empowerment, choice-making, service delivery, care giving and receiving, as well as many other ideas, norms and principles which stem from greatly different norm-systems, such as the ideal-type bureaucracy, the market and psychology. However, when going through the vast amount of research that examines the encounter between citizens and welfare workers, there seems to be two branches of overlapping research traditions, which rarely intertwine despite their objectives of study (the welfare encounter) being similar.

While writing this book, I have had a pile of literature for each of these research traditions sitting on my desk, literature that respectively centres the analysis of how bureaucratic principles affect the welfare encounter and how values stemming from a market context, standards of New Public Management (NPM) and norms from psychology influence the encounter. However, after going through many of these studies I am left with the impression that the focus of much of this research primarily reflects scholarly traditions and fails to adequately take into account the complexities of the empirical world. Political scientists seem to prefer the Weberian-inspired literature on the bureaucracy, for instance, the work of Michael Lipsky, whereas sociologists and anthropologists seem to prefer a critical Foucauldian-inspired approach that investigates the effects of market values, NPM and norms from psychology on the welfare encounter. Nevertheless, welfare workers and citizens adhere in reality to a wide range of norms and principles stemming from the bureaucracy, as well as the market and psychology, which is why an important goal of this book has been to engage with both branches of literature. By doing so, it is possible to produce analyses that explain what goes on in real-life welfare encounters. The applied theories and concepts of researchers have profound effects on what can be perceived, and they consequently affect the results of the analyses. If one applies a bureaucratic Lipsky-inspired approach, the result is then likely to be convincing analyses of discretionary practices. Similarly, if one applies Foucauldian conceptualisations, one will get convincing analyses of the subtle workings of power, which leaves very little room for the agency of welfare workers and citizens alike.

Having a background within anthropology and consequently favouring the analysis of the empirical world while simultaneously being a sociologist who is greatly inspired by a constructionist approach that acknowledges the role of theories and theoretical concepts for any analysis, I wish to apply both research traditions, and in doing so bridge two academic approaches which are rarely combined. I do so because it is my conviction, based on my own empirical studies and the reading of much research by my colleagues, that welfare encounters display principles of bureaucracy as well as values of the market, NPM and norms from psychology. By combining these two research traditions, my hope is to produce more convincing analyses than if each of these traditions were applied on their own. I will let the readers decide whether my endeavour has been successful.

I want to extend my largest gratitude for valuable help with the book to my colleagues at The Danish National Centre of Social Research (SFI) and the Department of Organization (Copenhagen Business School), my student assistant Charlotte Bossen Nielsen, Tony Mason, Robert Byron and the anonymous reviewers at Manchester University Press. Finally and of central importance for this book, I want to thank Professor Mark Haugaard, the editor of the series *Social and Political Power*, in which this book is part, whose insight into key power discussions has tremendously qualified the analyses and arguments of this book.

Nanna Mik-Meyer,
Copenhagen, October 2016

1

Introduction

Since the 1990s, European welfare states have undergone substantial changes regarding their objectives, areas of intervention and instruments of use (Bonoli and Natali 2012; Jenson 2012). Throughout the past three decades, there has been an increasing move away from a more classical understanding of government (hierarchical, top-down politics) to governance (cooperative, bottom-up politics), in other words a move towards the prioritisation of the involvement of citizens and the participation of civil society (Brugnoli and Colombo 2012: xi). This shift towards governance – and the inclusion of a more complex network of agencies in welfare work – has challenged the former dominant status of the bureaucracy in public institutions (Goss 2001: 1). Not only has this change altered the ways in which welfare work is organised, but it has in addition affected the encounter between citizens and professionals/welfare workers.

This books focuses on the altered (powerful) conditions for encounters between citizens and welfare workers. However, the three key concepts of citizen, professional and welfare worker need to be defined up front. The concept of citizen refers to civilians who encounter the welfare state, not because of their professional work identities as teachers, lawyers, doctors, social workers, technicians and so on, but because they have a social problem that requires help or attention from the welfare state. The concept of social problems refers to the idea that citizens do not only encounter welfare workers because of issues, which most would identify as actual problems (such as unemployment, illness and homelessness). They also encounter welfare workers with issues that need to be resolved but are not necessarily problems per se (such as school children who need extra attention or educational efforts, or citizens with disabilities who require tailored job arrangements).

The concept of citizen is inspired by Taylor-Gooby (2010) and his work on social citizenship, that is, the composition of citizenship at different periods of time and in different social contexts. Moreover, the analyses of the book are highly influenced by research that explores how the definition of the social problems of citizens as something to be resolved by the welfare state changes in accordance with these shifting contexts (e.g., Spector and Kitsuse 2001; Järvinen and Mik-Meyer 2003; Gubrium and Järvinen 2014a). The behavioural expectations of citizens are thus not a fixed entity but are being reframed by, for instance, shifting policies, legislation and societal norms and values, which all (re)define what it means to be a citizen and what constitutes a social problem that must be resolved by the welfare state in a particular social context at a particular time in history.

The concepts of professional and welfare worker also require extra attention. The reason for giving priority to the concept of welfare workers is to (also) engage with the work of individuals who do not have any formal educational training, for instance, people who work in similar employment positions as professions/professionals and who are regarded as part of an occupational group by their co-workers, clients, patients and so forth. Social workers and abuse consultants are examples of two groups of welfare workers who may have very different educational backgrounds but who nevertheless do similar work. The reason for not emphasising the educational background or training of staff members who encounter citizens also relates to the hypothesis that educational background and training are less important to the analysis and understanding of citizens' encounters with the welfare state. As this book will investigate, it may rather be the principles of the bureaucracy, values of the market and norms from psychology which one must highlight and foreground when analysing the powerful encounter between citizens and welfare workers.

Welfare work is not (only) about the legal rights of citizens but in addition involves servicing citizens, securing consumer responsiveness, user participation, cooperation and so on, which, in turn, affect this encounter (Goss 2001). Similarly, marketisation elements such as competition and freedom of choice also impact the relationship between citizens and welfare workers (Fotaki 2011). For this reason, work by fellow scholars with a particular interest in the conditions of the welfare encounter will be included. How bureaucratic principles (Chapter 5), market values (Chapter 6) and norms from psychology (Chapter 7) affect both the welfare encounter and the ways in which the participants perceive and understand the social problems of citizens are discussed. Also covered are the goals of welfare work today.

This book is particularly devoted to the dilemmas and paradoxes of present-day welfare work. This is reflected in the discussion of how (at this point in time) one can define the legitimacy of welfare work, how power is played out in welfare encounters and who may be regarded as a 'good citizen' according to the current fuzzy parameters of responsibility, individual autonomy and activeness (Goss 2001: 4; Lister 2001; Pykett *et al.* 2010).

In a British context, an approach to welfare work that centres around responsibility, individual autonomy, activeness and so on has been conceptualised as a Third Way approach to governance. This approach seeks to construct citizens as moral subjects who are active and responsible, as well as communities as responsible and strong units that actively engage in solving the problems of its citizens (Rose 2000). Third Way governance thus aims at transforming social problems – or 'public ills' – into 'ethical and cultural subjectivities' (Rose 2000: 1404), which is why Rose (2000) suggests that this type of governance should not be regarded as merely a political programme aimed at solving practical problems; it is in addition a programme designed to resolve the ethical and moral problems of presumably passive citizens and communities who are believed to be unaccustomed to taking responsibility for solving their own problems and those of their citizens, respectively. The underlying assumption of the Third Way approach is that 'those who refuse to become responsible and govern themselves ethically have also refused the offer to become members of our moral community', as Rose (2000: 1404, 1407) puts it.

Another way of framing this development from government to governance is by using the concepts of co-production, empowerment and user participation and involvement within public governance (e.g., Cahn 2000; Newman *et al.* 2004; Cowden and Singh 2007; Renedo and Marston 2014). Co-production, active citizenship, co-responsibilisation, user participation and user involvement (Newman and Tonkens 2011a; Evers and Guillemard 2013) are all concepts used to highlight the importance of engaging the citizen in welfare work. However, even though these concepts suggest individuality (to take responsibility for one's own situation, to act on one's opinions, etc.), they may instead be seen as powerful catchphrases, as they are used to prevent certain behaviours and encourage others. From a power perspective, these concepts work precisely because they disguise the fact that the freedom of the citizen is framed by very particular ideas of how to engage in active citizenship, responsibilisation and so forth.

Co-production is, for instance, used to emphasise involvement at both an individual level and at a societal level. At an individual level, a co-production approach seeks to make citizens feel that they are a needed and valued party in the design and implementation of welfare work. On a societal level, the co-production approach seeks to change the status of the citizen in the encounter with welfare workers. Instead of citizens being perceived as subordinate and dependent on the decisions of welfare workers, citizens and welfare workers should – from a co-production perspective – seek to actively create a relationship of 'parity, mutuality and reciprocity' with one another (Cahn 2000: 33–35). Co-production is thus an approach that simultaneously draws on ideas from psychology (Chapter 7) and market values (Chapter 6) in its dual focus on the presumable (psychological) needs of the citizens and the wish for a reciprocal relationship between citizens and welfare worker based on equality, capability to make choices and so on, expectations which greatly resemble those of the service encounter relationships in a market context (Cahn 2000: 146–147). However, and similar to the critique of the Third Way, the co-production, empowerment or user involvement approach is also criticised for being an imaginary model with no resemblance or transferability to real life. Cowden and Singh (2007: 18) explain:

> The story we are being told here is that in the bad old days Users would simply be told what to do by Professionals, whereas now there are all sorts of opportunities Users have for being involved in the services which are after all, run in their interest. This story is in fact imaginary because the decisions about how users can and should be involved are all controlled by professionals on one hand, and by the government and welfare bureaucracy on the other.

Even though there seems to be an extensive (political) wish to involve citizens in the management and resolution of their problems, this new involvement may still be regarded as, in fact, controlled by welfare workers, the government and/or the principles of the bureaucracy (Rose 2000; Clarke 2005; Clarke *et al.* 2007; Cowden and Singh 2007). In conclusion, social citizenship is currently being reframed, and with it the assumptions and beliefs about citizens today (Taylor-Gooby 2010). Key tasks for present-day welfare states are not only, for instance, the development of policies for unemployment and retirement (even though these are, of course, important assignments) but in addition the taking on of new assignments, such as caring for children and the elderly, securing equal opportunities between the sexes (Taylor-Gooby 2004; Bonoli 2005) and engaging in new types of relationships with its citizens, as captured by the concepts of Third Way governance, co-production, empowerment and personalisation (Whitaker 1980; Rose 2000; Needham 2008; Needham and Glasby 2015). These changing assumptions and beliefs in Western societies about the citizen entail that the citizen must be perceived as an expert on his or her situation, which, in turn, greatly impacts how the welfare worker is expected to encounter the citizen – and vice versa.

The present book takes a critical approach to these tendencies in today's welfare work of servicing and involving citizens as experts. This critical approach is based on an interactionist research approach (Chapter 4) to the discussion and analysis of the encounter between citizens and welfare workers. An interactionist approach places great analytical emphasis upon relations, that is, relations between citizens and welfare workers (e.g., their perceptions of each other and how these affect the welfare work), as well as those between dominant norms in society and organisations and people's own perceptions of their work and problems, respectively. The (professional) identities of welfare workers, as well as the identities of citizens (in the roles of, e.g., clients, patients or students), are formed and produced in particular societal and organisational contexts. Furthermore, the relations between welfare workers and citizens are inherently powerful, as they are based on legislative and administrative procedures of how to address the problems of citizens. Moreover, the encounter is powerful because it is influenced and governed by other resources, such as the dominant expectations of 'appropriate' behaviour that are linked to the moral norms within a particular welfare field, resources to which not all participants have access (Bourdieu 1998, 2011; Jenkins 2013).

From my own research on the changing roles of citizens and welfare workers in present-day welfare encounters (Järvinen and Mik-Meyer 2003, 2012; Mik-Meyer 2009, 2010b, 2011, 2014; Mik-Meyer and Villadsen 2014) and from the extensive literature reviews of fellow scholars on this area of research (e.g., Clarke et al. 2007; Lipsky 2010; Fotaki 2011; Needham 2011), it is clear that today's welfare encounters are dominated by bureaucratic principles, market values and norms from psychology (see also Chapter 8). Therefore, central questions, which this book seeks to answer, are how do the principles of the bureaucracy (e.g., rule-abiding conduct, equality, impartiality and legal certainty), the values of the market (e.g., service, freedom of choice, competition, entrepreneurial spirit, standards and benchmarks) and the norms from psychology (e.g., facilitation, coaching, emphatic and empowering efforts) affect the encounter with the citizen, and which challenges does the coexistence of these principles and norms produce?

The aim of this book is therefore to investigate the power of these principles, norms and values, because they prompt the use of specific resources or capitals, they are agenda-setting and they are sometimes attractive for both welfare workers and citizens. For instance, frequently used opposition pairs, such as active versus passive welfare policies, and welfare to work versus welfare dependency, are powerful catchphrases and contribute to reform and establish particular agendas within the public sector. In addition, these ideas and catchphrases lead to a particular perception of citizenship that requires further examination (Lister 2001).

The constitution of a 'good citizen' in today's welfare work thus involves descriptions of persons who engage in cooperative, active and responsible relations with welfare workers, descriptions that are defined and understood in particular societal and organisational contexts and which reflect particular understandings of authority (Pykett *et al.* 2010: 533). So even though any perception of the good citizen must be regarded as essentially a performative or enacted phenomenon, this performance or enactment is always related to a particular framework, dominating norms and so forth, which affects the encounter between citizens and the welfare state (Pykett *et al.* 2010: 533).

Based on the ways in which New Labour talks about citizens in the UK, Clarke suggests categorising citizenship according to four key aspects: activation, empowerment, responsibility and abandonment (Clarke 2005: 448–454). The activated citizens are citizens who are free of the pacifying state. The empowered citizens are citizens who – similar to consumers – are able to make choices and voice their situations; 'independent agents, rather than dependent subjects waiting on the state's whims' (Lister 2001; Clarke 2005: 450). The responsibilised citizens are moralised citizens whose choices and behaviours are reasonable, that is, 'responsible citizens make reasonable choices – and therefore "bad choices" result from the wilfulness of irresponsible people, rather than the structural distribution of resources, capacities and opportunities' (Clarke 2005: 451). Finally, the abandoned citizens are citizens who have been left behind by the state and may be perceived as the victims of the current developments of welfare states, which, for instance, render particular areas of welfare work (and their citizens) as no longer the responsibility of the welfare state (Clarke 2005: 454).

However, to address the ways in which citizens are perceived in today's encounter with welfare workers, the book will engage in discussions of power (Chapter 3) because ideas such as being active and responsible and making responsible choices may alter the power–knowledge relations between citizens and welfare workers (Newman and Tonkens 2011b: 179). When trying to ensure that citizens take on an active role and act responsibly to solve their problems, both citizens and welfare workers are then positioned in ways that render certain actions and perceptions 'natural' and others not. Note that the word *natural* has been placed in quotation marks, as no action or perception is natural in and of itself. The ways in which an act or utterance are perceived as a natural, obvious or normal way of behaving, reacting or perceiving the actions of others are by definition contextual and therefore related to particular dominant norms. Thus, norms are powerful, as they (and their particular context) enable the categorisation of certain actions as natural and obvious and others as strange, peculiar and abnormal.

The concept of power must therefore emphasise efficacy and resources (Jenkins 2013), which includes an investigation of how the different (symbolic) capitals of a particular welfare field affect the perceptions and actions of agents (Bourdieu 1998: 41; 2011), which – in turn – affects their (strategic) interaction (Goffman 1970). Furthermore, the book will use the concept of soft power, which was first developed by Nye in relation to the research field of international relations and which places great emphasis on agency (1990). There are three reasons for using this concept. Firstly, soft power is defined in opposition to coercive power and thus reflects the goal of investigating both negative and positive aspects of power relations within welfare encounters and welfare work, with a particular emphasis on agency. Secondly, soft power is a well-known and widely used concept within international relations; however, the concept has received little attention outside this research field, which makes it a less loaded concept, as it lacks the many preconceptions and connotations of other similar concepts of power, such as three-dimensional (3-D) power as investigated by Lukes (2005) and four-dimensional (4-D) discursive power as investigated by Foucault (1983). Soft power thus concerns the shaping of both epistemic perceptions (3-D) and social constructions of social subjects (4-D). Finally, the linguistic qualities of the term *soft power* in and of itself produces expectations of power relations that are both soft (i.e., gentle, kind and indulgent) and powerful or hard, as such relations – despite their soft nature – structure and dominate the encounter between citizens and welfare workers.

Investigations of power processes need to address both structural elements (such as the norms and principles at play in the encounter between the welfare worker and the citizen) and the agency of the participants who act and make choices, even when constrained by norms and principles of welfare work. The goal is to contribute to familiar discussions of power and (professional) work, but to do so from a different vantage point, one that provides a new explanatory frame for how the two relate. The concept of soft power allows for the investigations of both the ways in which individuals manipulate each other in an effort to achieve their desired goals (3-D) and how the resources of the investigated field both affect and bias certain individuals (4-D).

Finally, there is a need for clarifying and discussing the concept of the welfare state used in the present book, as it draws on examples of welfare work from very different nation states within this same category of welfare state, despite the differences between these nations. The book includes research from countries that are often believed to belong to very different welfare models, such as the UK, the US, Australia, Scotland, Germany, France, the Netherlands, Sweden and Denmark. These countries are rarely presented together, as they are often categorised as belonging to Anglo-Saxon, Continental or Nordic welfare models. However, because a main goal is to analyse how principles of the bureaucracy, values of the market and norms from psychology affect the encounter between citizens and welfare workers, the empirical similarities of these various welfare states (e.g., fertility rates, educational spending, level of employment, housing taxes and inequality) are of less importance here.[1] Rather, the choice of which analyses to include has depended on whether the studies in question included analyses of how different principles, norms and values affected the encounter between welfare workers and citizens.

The goal of the book is thus to investigate trends across very diverse welfare areas and not first and foremost to deliver a more detailed analysis of particular welfare areas (education, social work, employment, etc.). This level of analysis is of course both an interesting and important area of research; nevertheless, it falls outside the scope of this current endeavour.

The book consists of three main sections: Part I discusses – in greater detail than in the present introduction – extracts from state-of-the-art research on professions and expertise (Chapter 2), the perception of power that guides the analyses (Chapter 3) and the overall theoretical positioning when analysing encounters between welfare workers and citizens as co-productive and interactionist (Chapter 4).

Part II presents a number of analyses that can be organised in accordance with three sets of principles and norms which impact the encounters between welfare workers and citizens today: firstly, analyses that show how a bureaucratic context affects the encounter between – in this case – administrators and clients (Chapter 5); secondly, analyses that show how a market context affects the encounter between – in this case – service providers and consumers/customers (Chapter 6); and thirdly, analyses that show how a psychology-inspired context affects the encounter between – in this case – coaches and coachees (Chapter 7). All three contexts are to be perceived as Weberian ideal types, in other words, theoretical constructs based on observations of the real world, which nevertheless cannot be regarded as actually mirroring the empirical world in precise detail or in any particular instance.

Lastly, Part III contains two chapters, the first of which presents two detailed analyses of encounters between welfare workers and citizens, with particular emphasis on the role of the principles of the bureaucracy, the norms from psychology and the values of the market in the welfare encounter (Chapter 8). The final chapter (Chapter 9) summarises the key points of the book.

Overall, the book seeks to delineate how welfare workers are not merely acting in accordance with a professional code of ethics, as studies show that they also engage in (often conflicting) assignments of administrating, service providing and coaching citizens who are consequently expected to act in accordance with their multifaceted roles as clients, consumers and expert citizens.

Note

1. For an updated comparison of these issues, see Bonoli and Natali's (2012) recently edited monograph.

Part I

Power and professions in welfare work

2

Professions, de-professionalisation and welfare work

Introduction

As stated in the introduction, the concept of welfare worker makes it possible to analyse the encounter between citizens and a broad group of people: those who have both long (professionals) and short (semi-professionals) educations, as well as employees without any formal training for conducting welfare work. An important feature – and common denominator – of these people is that their work lives involve (or even revolve around) encounters with citizens in welfare institutions, encounters influenced by organisational and societal principles and norms, that is, Durkheimian social facts (1982). Another aligned feature of their work lives is that their position and expert knowledge – regardless if this expert knowledge stems from their educational backgrounds or work experiences – can be seen as a form of social control that affects the welfare work, as well as the encounter with the citizen.

However, and as many scholars have noted, the concepts of profession, professionals, professionalisation and so forth can be quite problematic in a number of ways (e.g., Evetts 2011; Atkinson 2014; Freidson 2014). For instance, Atkinson (2014: 185) argues that neither the dominant functionalist approach to professions nor the interactionist perception of professions and educational knowledge is able to examine how the education of welfare workers, their practice and the organisation of the work relate, even though there is no doubt that professions and educational knowledge are connected (Atkinson 2014: 185). Freidson (2014: 25) voices a similar critique and urges scholars to be very cautious of their use of the term *professional* (and variations hereof). Although this reservation about the use of the concepts of professions, professionals and so on is important, it is nevertheless necessary for analyses of welfare encounters to engage with some of the discussions put forth in the extensive research fields of the sociology of professions (e.g., Abbott 1988, 2001;

Dingwall and Lewis 2014), professionalisation (e.g., Evetts 2003, 2011; Freidson 2004) and expertise (e.g., Dreyfus and Dreyfus 2005; Carr 2010; Eyal 2013) – not least the work that explicitly focuses on contextual and relational matters, such as the effect of various norm-systems on the work of professions or professionals.

An important context is, for instance, how expertise acts as a social control that organises the welfare work (Rueschemeyer 2014: 32). This argument rests on the assumption that the recipients of expert services are neither able to solve their problems on their own nor in a position to assess the nature or quality of the service provided to them (Rueschemeyer 2014: 31). Nevertheless, one can argue the same for welfare workers who are also subjected to this type of relational social control, as the expectations of both their managers and clients or patients, whom they seek to help or provide a service to, as well as the formal legislations (and other structural factors), also organise and govern the (work) lives of these people. The point is that the context is crucial in defining who will be positioned as an expert and who will not. According to Rueschemeyer (2014: 35),

> the power balance between expert practitioners and the major groups with which they deal is tilted to the disadvantage of the [traditional] experts so that consumers or third parties can define their needs for service relatively independent and ... can control the quality of performance of the practitioners.

In other words, one can no longer assume that the welfare workers are automatically positioned as experts in the encounter with citizens. It may instead be the citizens who are placed as the experts of their own lives and needs, and thus the citizens who set the agenda in the welfare encounter. Or it may even be a political agenda with its corresponding principles and rules of how to conduct 'good welfare work' that determines what may count as meaningful and appropriate behaviour of welfare workers (and citizens). Chapter 8 examines both of these power processes.

Due to the overarching focus on how principles, norms and values – originating elsewhere than the particular disciplinary fields of the welfare workers – affect the encounter between citizens and welfare workers, it is primarily scholarly work that contributes to what Freidson (2004: 2) calls the third logic of professionalism that will be discussed here. The third logic of professionalism is a set of assumptions that differs from (and can even be regarded as in conflict with) the logics of both the bureaucracy and the market. Even though the focus of this book is similar to that of Freidson, he takes a more classic approach to the analysis of professions. He examines how the logics of the free market and the bureaucracy work in very different ways than the logic of professions, as the market and the bureaucracy automatically position the consumers and the managers, respectively, as in control. Conversely, the main focus here is on the *influence* of the logics or rationales of the bureaucracy and the market (similar to Freidson), as well as the rationales of psychology, and to discuss how these three set of rationales affect present-day welfare encounters.

Evetts' (2009a, 2009b) distinction between occupational professionalism (governed by professional norms) and organisational professionalism (governed by organisational norms) will also be further discussed. The aim of this particular distinction is to illustrate and point to a development in which one kind of professionalism (one that emphasises aspects of trust in the education of the professionals) is currently being dominated by a new kind of professionalism influenced by the bureaucracy's focus on proce-dures and routines and the market's focus on performance measures. This new kind of professionalism not only affects the encounter between profes-sionals and citizens; it changes it completely (Evetts 2011: 412, 416), as this kind of professionalism is saturated with principles of regulation and control (Liljegren 2012: 297). However, the chapter begins with a brief overview of a few key themes within the sociology of professions, which are particularly relevant for analyses of welfare encounters (e.g., Abbott 1988; Dingwall and Lewis 2014). This short presentation is followed by a discus-sion of the scholarly literature that centres around how norms outside the professional disciplines affect the work of the professionals (e.g., Broadbent *et al.* 1997; Freidson 2004; Noordegraaf 2007; Evetts 2009a; Liljegren 2012). Finally, the chapter concludes by discussing the work of scholars who address the subject matters of expertise, de-professionalisation and power within welfare work (e.g., Dreyfus and Dreyfus 2005; Duyvendak *et al.* 2006; Carr 2010; Eyal 2013).

The sociology of professions

According to Dingwall (2014), most of the current research on the sociology of professions draws on either the studies of Parsons, in which he investigated the social foundation of knowledge within medicine and medical practices, or the work of Hughes and his particular interest in the (strong) mandate of the professions. As opposed to the then dominant economic approach to the individual as essentially utilitarian and calcu-lating, Parsons revealed in his studies on medicine and medical practice that individuals within organisations possessed a shared collegial orienta-tion to their work. This finding could, in other words, not be explained by the model of the economic man, a self-interested, self-maximising individ-ual. If one were to understand the actions and behaviours of, for instance, doctors and nurses, it was instead the socially grounded normative order of medicine that had to take centre-stage in the analysis (Dingwall 2014: 2).

Hughes focused in particular on the licence and mandate of the professions, meaning that certain occupations have licence to perform certain actions in exchange for money, and if these workers in addition possess a sense of community through either shared work experiences or education, then they are also 'likely to claim a mandate to define, for themselves and others, proper conduct in relation to their work' (Dingwall 2014: 4). For Hughes (and Hughes-inspired research), professions are an illustrative example of a group of individuals with a strong mandate who can be studied through ethnographic methods. Through their common training within a particular field, this group of people is not only assumed to know how best to resolve problems, issues and so forth within their particular field of work; they are also allowed to define how to think about the problems within their domain. Professions and professionalism therefore have to do with both technical and moral aspects. Technically, professions are thought of as competent in their use of complex knowledge that requires a formal education, and morally, professions are expected not only to solve the problems at hand with their technical expertise but also to be the only ones who can be trusted to do the work (Brint 1994: 7).

Even though one can regard the classic approaches of Parsons and Hughes to the study of profession as different from each other in a number of ways (e.g., in relation to their definitions of profession and norms and their impact on the work of professions), the two scholars both believed that there was indeed a need to engage with how the professions are affected by outside factors, such as principles from the market and from business, a research focus that in the 1970s and 1980s was still very much neglected (Dingwall 2014: 6). Thus, professions and professionals were already in the 1970s and 1980s seen as 'historically evolving sociological forms' (Brint 1994: 4), which relied on the definition of formal knowledge at that time, that is, the prevailing or dominant (political) perception of what it takes to be a profession or a professional.

However, not all scholars saw (and still see) professions as historically evolving sociological forms. Some scholars thus condemn the context and practice in their definition (and analysis) of professions and therefore obstruct systematic research anchored in empirical and intellectual analysis (see Freidson's [2014: 14–15] critique hereof). Scholars have attempted to resolve this static and de-contextualised way of engaging with the definition of professions by focusing solely on the process of professionalisation. This change of term, however, still does not solve the problem of definition, as pointed out by several scholars (e.g., Sciulli 2005; Torstendahl 2005), as – arguably – one cannot study a process well without having a definition (or here, a profession) guiding the focus (Freidson 2014: 15). For this reason, Freidson (2014: 16) suggests to view professions as a changing historical concept. The medieval universities of Europe produced, for instance, only three professions (doctors, lawyers and men of the clergy), which by Elliott were defined as status professions (Freidson 2014: 16–17). The choice of only regarding three occupations as actual professions was challenged in nineteenth-century England (and later on in the US), where many middle-class occupations also made claims to the title of profession (Freidson 2014: 17).[1] However, and as shown by later scholarly work, the idea of professions as a status category is currently being challenged by the fact that the work of professionals is increasingly being governed by market and organisational aspects: 'powerful social and economic forces have brought the older idea of professionalism linking social purposes and knowledge-based authority close to an end', as Brint (1994: 17) argues.

Earlier work on professions also includes Abbott's classic book *The System of Professions* (1988), in which he examines central questions about the role of professions in modern life. By comparing professions in the UK, France, and the US in the nineteenth and twentieth centuries, he develops a general theory of professions and how they progress. Abbott argues that professions dominate outsiders through the control of knowledge and its application; they have their own interdependent systems by which each profession has its activities under various kinds of jurisdictions. Professions are consequently either in full control or subordinate to other profession groups. For this reason, Abbott (1988: 2) claims that it is essential to study the jurisdiction (and jurisdictional disputes) of a given profession, as the practical authority of any profession is based on its systems of knowledge. Professions evolve because of their interrelations, which at the same time are governed by their control of both knowledge and skill. Abbott uses the concept of abstraction to define (and illustrate) the cornerstone of a profession, namely, that practical skills arise from having an abstract system of knowledge (Abbott 1988: 8). In this classic text, he argues that any occupation can obtain a licence or develop a code of ethics, but only occupations based on an abstract system of knowledge are able or allowed to (re)define problems and tasks and thus take their place within the competitive system of professions (Abbott 1988: 8–9).

Similar to many other scholars, Abbott was also interested in researching professionalisation, or the patterns of the development of professions (Abbott 1988: 9). However, and according to Abbott, the (at the time) previous theories of professionalisation were all anchored in either a functional model (with focus on how professions can control the asymmetrical expert–client relation), a structural model (with focus on the structural and historical developments of professions), a monopolist model (with focus on dominance, authority and larger external social processes, such as the rise of the bureaucracy) or a cultural model (with focus on the cultural legitimacy and authority, as well as expertise, as a social relation) (Abbott 1988: 15). From Abbott's perspective, similar to the perspectives of Parson and Hughes, all these theories are too preoccupied with structural elements rather than the actual work of the professions: 'It is the content of the professions' work that the case studies tell us is changing. ... By switching from a focus on the organisational structures of professions to a focus on groups with common work we replace several of the problematic assumptions at once' (Abbott 1988: 19–20). In his own analyses of American medicine and how professions within this field acted and interrelated, psychiatry stood out because the professions of this field were actually rooted in an organisation (and not a specific education). In studying law professionals in England and France, as well as accountants in England, Abbott not only revealed the breath-taking diversity of professional life; he also illustrated how professions were pursuing jurisdiction and control and exhibited an urge to defeat rival or competing professions (Abbott 1988: 21, 23, 30). In his own words,

> the organizational formalities of professions are meaningless unless we understand their context. This context always relates back to the power of the professions' knowledge systems, their abstracting ability to define old problems in new ways. Abstraction enables survival. (Abbott 1988: 30)

As argued by Abbott (and Parson and Hughes for that matter), analyses of encounters in welfare institutions have to engage with the contexts of the work. This work is inhabited by diverse professions and semi-professions, such as lawyers, doctors, nurses, teachers, social workers and pedagogues (and staff without professional training), and is moreover influenced by both formal and informal social structures – the social facts (Durkheim 1982). However, context implies different factors than professional knowledge (as suggested in the above quote by Abbott), as one cannot assume that context will always be related 'back to the power of the professionals' knowledge systems'. The governing contextual factors are neither necessarily nor first and foremost the knowledge systems of the professions. The governing contextual factors might rather be the dominating norm-systems existing outside the professional knowledge systems, which affect the encounter between citizens and welfare workers (who may or may not belong to a profession).

The point is not that the knowledge systems of professions and the battles between competing knowledge systems are not important or relevant to the research of these encounters. Similarly, the point is not to argue that 'all occupations – whether casual day-labour, assembly-line work, teaching, surgery or systems analysis – are so much alike that there is no point in making distinctions of any kind', as Freidson (2014: 15) aptly critiques certain scholars for implicitly doing when they refuse to define what they mean by occupation and profession. It makes a difference whether the citizen is encountering, for instance, a doctor, a nurse or the nurse's assistant when seeking help for a medical problem. However, the main goal of the coming analyses is to shed light on a slightly different phenomenon in the encounter and explore how other norm-systems influence the encounter between the welfare worker and the citizen. It goes without saying that the impact of principles and norms on individuals – be they welfare workers or citizens – will vary according to the educational backgrounds (professions) of the individuals, their experiences and a number of other factors, as shown in the large research field of the sociology of professions.

Organisational professionalism versus occupational professionalism

As illustrated so far, the concepts of profession and professionalisation (and how they differ) have been much debated. Scholars have similarly engaged in lengthy debates about these concepts in an effort to shed light on how one can understand the role of professions today. Evetts (2003, 2006, 2009a, 2009b, 2011), for instance, has written extensively on what constitutes professionalism and puts forth the notion of two ideal types of professionalism in knowledge-based work: organisational professionalism and occupational professionalism (Evetts 2009a: 263, 2009b). Organisational professionalism is, among other things, defined by managerial control, a rational-legal type of authority, standardised procedures, a hierarchical decision-making structure and performance reviews, and is linked to the Weberian ideal-type bureaucracy. Occupational professionalism is, on the other hand, characterised primarily by the professional groups being in control, a collegial authority, discretion and occupational control of the work, trust in practitioners, monitored professional ethics and so forth and is associated with a Durkheimian (ideal-type) model of occupational communities (for further elaboration, see model 1 in Evetts 2009a).

One must bear in mind that both types of professionalisms are ideal types and that actual welfare encounters most often involve what Liljegren (2012: 309) has called pragmatic professionalism, in which staff combine the rationales of their work organisation with those of their occupational backgrounds. Evetts makes a slightly different argument, although by naming them ideal types she also seeks to remind the reader that neither type of professionalism can be found in its purest form in practice. She argues, however, that a governing technology such as New Public Management (NPM) actually brings about its own unique type of professionalism that differs greatly from the two ideal types of organisational professionalism and occupational professionalism.

This third type of professionalism, the NPM professionalism, emphasises a different type of control than what is associated with the ideal-type bureaucracy (Weber) or the ditto occupational communities (Durkheim). NPM is a governing technology that centres around community control and involves the complex interplay between many different agencies and interests, which means that the worker thus changes roles from a professional to that of a manager (Evetts 2009a: 255). Similar to Evetts, it is neither the work of Weber on the bureaucracy and its procedures nor the work of Durkheim on social facts and occupational communities that will be the focus of this chapter. It instead focuses solely on why it is important to discuss professionalism in a different way today when investigating what goes on in (professional) work organisations. Evetts writes,

> If the focus of analysis is shifted away from the concepts of profession (as a distinct and generic category of occupational work) and professionalization (as the process to pursue, develop and maintain the closure of the occupational group) and towards the concept of professionalism, then different kinds of explanatory theory become apparent. Then the discourse of professionalism can be analysed as a powerful instrument of occupational change and social control at macro, meso and micro levels and in a wide range of occupations in very different work, organizational and employment relations, contexts and conditions. (Evetts 2009b: 20)

The point is that the concepts of profession and professionalisation are today being used about various kinds of workers and various types of work, both of which do not necessarily fit with the classic definition with focus on jurisdictions or what it takes to be a professional or conduct professional work (Evetts 2009a, b: 19). For this reason, she suggests the concept of professionalism, which calls for a different kind of explanatory theory, one that may shed light on, for instance, power relations within a wide range of occupations and within different work settings.

According to Evetts, the professionalism of most contemporary public service occupations is imposed from above from the employers and managers of the professionals, such as the wish of managers for dedicated service and autonomous decision-making (Evetts 2009b: 22). It is, in other words, the (political) goals of the organisation which define the overall relationship between welfare workers and citizens (e.g., the expectations of welfare workers to be morally committed to their work) and set achievement targets and performance indicators. Consequently, these (political) goals may, in fact, govern the interactions between welfare workers and citizens in a new way that does not leave (much) room for the exercise of professional, disciplinary-based discretion and as a result hinders the ethics of the profession to come into play (Evetts 2009b: 23–24).

Thus, the ways in which welfare workers are regulated today may not stem primarily from occupational norms and ethics but rather from the normative expectations of society, for instance, the prioritisation of approaching the citizens from a place of empowerment, innovation and autonomy (Evetts 2009b: 26). Such principles and norms go hand in hand with a strong focus on the individual performance of not only citizens (in the roles of customers and/or expert citizens) but also welfare workers (in the roles of service providers and coaches). These principles and norms are in Evetts' (2009b: 26) words 'powerful mechanisms of worker/employee control in which occupational values of professionalism are used to promote the efficient management of the organization'. NPM professionalism and its focus on efficiency means that this type of professionalism is measured against the number of citizens receiving help – also on the expense of the help given to the individual person. Thus, the individual may receive a help that from a strictly professional ethos perspective is problematic but that nevertheless is preferable because this 'reduced' help secures the better of many citizens' situations.

This redefinition of what it means to be a professional and what it means to be working on behalf of a profession has resulted in a changing working relationship between welfare workers and citizens, a change in which the educational or occupational backgrounds of the welfare workers are perhaps less central. The present-day relationships between welfare workers and citizens are being transformed into, for instance, customer relations, as Chapter 6, which deals with principles and values from the market, will show: 'Clients are converted into customers and professional work competencies become primarily related to and defined and assessed by the work organization' (Evetts 2009b: 28). The argument is that management technologies such as NPM emphasise particular market principles, such as competition, individualisation and service engagement with clients (customer relations), and thereby suppress occupational norms stemming from the educational backgrounds or experiences of the welfare workers (Evetts 2009a: 253).

These work conditions do not only favour flexible specialisations of welfare workers (which, in turn, threaten professional autonomy) and work conditions that increasingly professionalise nonprofessional employees, such as consultants and managers (Noordegraaf 2007: 763). These work conditions also entail a particular perception of professionalism which both emphasises its contextualised and situated nature and (to a certain point) transforms professional work into a question of reclaiming lost occupational control (Noordegraaf 2007: 764). The so-called pure professionalism of the past that centres around disciplinary knowledge, skills and experience, jurisdictional control, knowledge transfer and codes of conduct is threatened by what is being termed a situated and hybridised form of professionalism that emphasises a reflexive form of control. This control is not so much about *'being* a professional as it is about *becoming* professional' (Noordegraaf 2007: 768, 771 – emphasis in the original).

Unlike pure or situated types of professionalism, the hybridised professionalism does not centre around occupational control (pure professionalism) or organisational control (situated professionalism) but emphasises instead a reflexive type of control, that is, the ability to form 'meaningful connections' between citizens and welfare workers (Noordegraaf 2007: 780). However, meaningful connections is an empirical construct that will necessarily vary from context to context and in accordance with the dominating norms of how to approach a citizen's problems in a meaningful way, how to perceive one's own problem in a meaningful way, how to behave as welfare workers and citizens in a meaningful way and how to define meaningful goals of the welfare work.

Even though the investigation of all these questions – in principal, at least – must be regarded as purely empirical questions (and therefore to be determined empirically), several authors have pointed out that there seem to be certain principles and norms that are quite persistent today and have been so for quite some time, which appear to organise the empirical world of social problems in a certain way. Therefore, when discussing what Broadbent and colleagues (1997: 2) call the fundamental rationale for professionalism, one must engage with both the diversity of professional practice and the changes in professionalism, which reflect their reactions to particular and overarching contextual changes. One important change in this regard – which is mentioned by many authors – is the engagement with the principles and values of neoliberalism and the following emphasis of individuality and rights linked to ownership. These values are at odds with the ways in which welfare workers used to define rights, as their definition was typically related to citizenship and not individual ownership.

These principles and values from neoliberalism can therefore be seen as confronting the previous power position of professionals. Their relatively autonomous knowledge position gave them the rights to define not only a problem but also its solution, and this position therefore entails a type of control that does not fit well with the new general emphasis on individuality (Broadbent *et al.* 1997: 6). In addition, changing technology and modes of organisation affect professionalism and professional autonomy as well (Broadbent *et al.* 1997: 10). According to Broadbent and colleagues, neoliberal values and new ways of organising work result in three issues or tensions in how professionalism may develop: firstly, professionals – this book's welfare workers – are caught in the tensions between their (professional) autonomy as experts and the control mechanisms of their work organisation. Secondly, professionals engage with both a (professional) expert identity and an organisational work identity that may emphasise other norms regarding meaningful behaviour, for instance, citizens as experts. Thirdly, professionals must respect the practices of their work organisations while simultaneously striving to change these practices (Broadbent *et al.* 1997: 10).

This development of the role of professions today, as well as the aforementioned tensions, may therefore make it relevant to ask again, as Wilensky (1964) did back in 1964, if everyone, in fact, is being professionalised. Are welfare workers (with technical competences, who adhere to norms of professional behaviour) to be regarded as professionals today? Or is the expertise of welfare workers being weakened due to a fundamentally changed work environment, which emphasises neoliberal values and perceives the individual in new ways? Wilensky identified in the 1960s what he termed a push towards professionalisation (1964: 142), but he also found that this so-called professionalisation of everyone was met with several barriers from organisations (their norms and procedures) and from professions with exclusive jurisdictions.

This meant that only few occupations in his study were able to achieve professional status and authority. For this reason, he concluded (in 1964) that future occupational groups would need to combine elements from both their professional background and the principles of the organisation (the bureaucratic context); the professional would, in other words, have to combine a professional and non-professional orientation to his or her work. Therefore, if the significant aspect for understanding the encounter between welfare workers and citizens is not whether the welfare worker is technically a professional, a semi-professional or a person without educational training, then a slightly different branch of literature becomes relevant, literature that addresses the concepts of experts and expertise and thus enables a different approach to discussions of welfare work.

The sociology of expertise and de-professionalisation

The research area of expertise is – like the sociology of professions – a large area of study. In this particular case, however, only the scholarly discussions of expertise that are of explicit relevance to (the powerful) encounter between welfare workers and citizens are included. Dreyfus and Dreyfus (2005: 779) employ a five-stage model of competence or skill – novice, advanced beginner, competence, proficiency and expert – of which the fifth and highest stage is that of expertise. By focusing particularly on accident prevention and medical expertise, Dreyfus and Dreyfus examine to what extent expertise may be captured in rule-based expert systems. They argue that given the historical development of expertise, scholars of today ought to take 'a fresh look' at the relationship between skills and expertise and suggest characterising expertise as a subtle and 'immediate intuitive situational response'; a beginner follows rules whereas the expert never follows rules but does 'what normally works and, of course, it normally works' (2005: 780, 787–788).

Central for the argument here is Dreyfus and Dreyfus' (2005) finding that rule-based expert systems are bound to fail, as such systems force the expert to regress to the level of a beginner. In applying this knowledge to the medical field, they find that strengthening the bureaucratisation and standardisation of organisations may have the unintended effect of lessening the level of skills and expertise in the organisation due to the over-reliance of the bureaucracy on a calculative rationality. As they argue, experts rely on intuition and not calculation, even when reflecting (Dreyfus and Dreyfus 2005: 790). Their work thus introduces the mismatch between expertise and the calculative rationality of the bureaucracy.

A recent paper by Eyal (2013) also deals explicitly with the matter of expertise and how the sociology of expertise differs from (and is complementary to) the sociology of professions. Here, expertise is understood and analysed as 'networks that link together objects, actors, techniques, devices, and institutional and spatial arrangements' (Eyal 2013: 864). As opposed to the sociology of professions in which jurisdiction takes centre-stage ('who has control and to what degree over a set of tasks'), Eyal (2013: 872) argues that the sociology of expertise rather considers which arrangements must be in place in order for staff to solve an assignment. However, the sociology of professions and the sociology of expertise must complement each other, as an accurate analysis of what happens in organisations will rely on a research design that combines knowledge of how networks of expertise are brought together with a jurisdictional analysis. This combination will, according to Eyal (2013: 877, 686), ensure an analysis of how problems are both defined and resolved.

There is a strong focus on networks (Eyal 2013: 899), 'gestures, uniforms and other visual media in the enactment of expertise' (Carr 2010: 19), within the sociology of expertise, which make this scholarly field quite different from the sociology of professions, which traditionally emphasises the educational background and other characteristics of the individual. An important point within the literature on expertise is that expertise is 'something people do rather than something people have or hold' (Carr 2010: 18), which is why the aspect of interaction becomes central to any such analyses. The literature on expertise emphasises how – in this case – welfare workers and citizens act within so-called hierarchies of values, which authorise and define certain ways of acting as an expert and thus govern the encounter between the two parties (Carr 2010: 18). For this reason, the (organisational) socialisation processes, such as (organisational) training and apprenticeship, become key, as it is within these socialisation processes that people learn to be(come) experts (Carr 2010: 19), welfare workers and citizens alike.

In the final part of this chapter, another set of themes related to the sociology of both professions and expertise is introduced, namely, the discussions of new professionalism (Duyvendak *et al.* 2006; Evetts 2011; Speed and Gabe 2013), re-professionalisation (Duyvendak *et al.* 2006) and de-professionalisation and how these characteristics may be regarded as inextricable consequences of the strong current influence of marketisation and managerialism on welfare work (Rogowski 2010). With particular reference to social work, Rogowski (2010: 111; see also Duyvendak *et al.* 2006) argues that the current emphasis on users as experts and user empowerment can be regarded as an attack on the expert position of social workers and thereby a threat to their professional autonomy. This user focus can be understood in light of the overall so-called de-professionalising tendency within social work.

Even though one can regard the transformation of social work into a graduate profession as a sign of increased professionalisation, the parallel and quite strong business tendency towards privatisation and marketisation of social work since the 1980s and 1990s, combined with more managerial control in the UK, has nevertheless – according to Rogowski – led to a de-professionalisation of social work (Rogowski 2010: 133–136). These neoliberal influences have, in other words, changed the very definitions of meaningful social work (Rogowski 2010: 136). These influences have led to a move away from the so-called bureau-professionalism of the past, a kind of professionalisation that combined a rational administration with professional discretion (as will be investigated in Chapter 5). Today's social work is dominated by a managerial kind of professionalisem. Within managerial social work, the preferred agents are managers rather than professionals or administrators, and this kind of professionalism is thus closely associated with the economic and political changes related to neoliberalism (Rogowski 2010: 138).

Strategies such as personalisation (see also Chapter 6) seek to make the recipients of welfare services take more responsibility for their situation. Citizens are now expected to choose, decide and shape their own lives, as argued by Rogowski (2010: 155). However, when social workers disagree with the choices and decisions of citizens, then their expertise and judgements are confronted and challenged. Techniques such as personalisation may therefore result in the acceptance and employment of unqualified social workers ('unreflective people-processors') who are both cheaper and easier to manage and control than educated social workers: 'They will, therefore, be more willing and able to tick choice-denying boxes rather than support users to achieve the best quality of life open to them, even if it is more expensive for the public purse' (Rogowski 2010: 155). Some scholars write about the so-called victims of neoliberalism, inferring that these instruments, principles and interventions may cause a division between front-line welfare workers and managers, which, in turn, creates an us and them culture in the workplace (Jones 2001: 559). Interventions conducted within settings dominated by neoliberal values will, for instance, be evidence based rather than reflecting the preferences and opinions of their workers (Rogowski 2010: 162, 184) and may therefore threaten the expertise of the front-line workers, regardless if they are part of a profession or semi-profession or have no formal training.

The argument of this branch of literature is that managers and policy-makers are so disconnected from the actual work of semi-professionals, such as teachers, policemen and social workers, that the work and decisions of managers and policymakers become foreign to the front-line welfare staff. The introduction of marketisation, accountability and user involvement to welfare work is seen as limiting of the roles available to semi-professionals in their encounters with citizens (Duyvendak *et al.* 2006: 7). Duyvendak and colleagues (2006) suggest the term *democratic professionalism* in order to pinpoint the particular effects of techniques, such as privatisation and the engagement of citizens, for instance, strategies of user involvement, empowerment and co-production. Democratic professionalism implies a different rationale than Freidson's (2004) logics of the professionals, the market or the bureaucracy, as the rationale of democratic professionalism is all about securing the voices of citizens without challenging the knowledge position of professionals. In its ideal form, this approach to the citizen is believed to ensure trust in the relationship between client and professional (Duyvendak *et al.* 2006: 13). However, and as Chapters 6 and 7 on the influence of market values and norms from psychology will also show, this may not always be the case, as not all citizens within welfare work can live up to this role of the knowledgeable, empowered and serviceable citizen (Duyvendak *et al.* 2006: 13). Similarly, welfare workers may also be challenged by the aim of securing the voices of citizens when (or if) these voicings actually confront basic perceptions of welfare workers.

Concluding comments

Expertise and professional norms are phenomena which derive meaning from the context in which they are produced. For this reason, there is no need to be too preoccupied with how to define a profession, as Evetts (2011: 396) suggests.

Professionals and semi-professionals of today are neither merely carrying a particular norm-system that (in a positive way) supports a normative social order, nor are they solely influenced by an ideology or 'hegemonic belief system' that (in a negative way) controls them (Evetts 2003: 399). One must therefore assume a third theoretical position that combines elements from the two other perspectives: namely, that professionals and semi-professionals may be perceived as having a 'distinctive form of decentralised occupational control which is important in civil society' (Evetts 2003: 403). Professionalism should be regarded as a unique form of occupational control. It is a form of control that differs from (and is superior to) those stemming from the market, the bureaucracy and the particular organisations. Evetts argues for a more pragmatic definition of the professions in which the differentiation between professions and experts is neither relevant nor important (Evetts 2006: 135), as today's professionalism is negotiated within particular contexts which favour certain ways of defining the social problems of citizens. These ways of defining the social problems of citizens are embedded in principles of the bureaucracy, the values of the market and the norms from psychology, remembering that encounters in practice do not showcase these principles, values and norms in their purest form.

This pragmatic definition of professions allows for the study of how professionalism relates to different norm-systems and how these contexts stimulate a particular social order and control. The label *professional* is perhaps just a 'piece of sociological material' Brint (1994: 8) that takes form according to the changing social and cultural contexts. To be a professional or a welfare worker is, therefore, perhaps not first and foremost about the functions perceived as central to the public welfare, but rather has to do with the particular contextual definitions of what is accepted as knowledge within a particular field at a certain time in history (Brint 1994: 8, 11). To regard professions and professionalism as knowledge-based authority systems has, in other words, long been a quite old-fashioned approach, as the dominance of economic factors, new ways of perceiving the citizen and his or her role in welfare work and new targets for welfare workers have brought about a very different setting for the encounter between citizens and welfare workers.

Note

1. For a more nuanced discussion of the historical roots of professions in Europe and the US, see Freidson (2014).

3

Soft power and welfare work

Introduction

Investigations of the encounter between welfare workers and citizens must use a concept of power that does not automatically privilege, for instance, the particular profession of welfare workers, as is done in much literature on professions. The concept of power must be based on a dialectic relationship between what can be called the objective structures and the subjective experiences of these structures (Giddens' [1984] concept of structuration). To situate analyses of welfare encounters within the structure–agency debate (e.g., Hayward and Lukes 2008) will emphasise both the structural conditions (such as legislation, economy and norm-systems; the resources of the field) and agency (the ways in which citizens and welfare workers create, interpret, manipulate and react to these structural conditions).

In recognising the critique of 'totalising theories of power' (Haugaard 1997), such as Foucauldian theory-laden analyses (which are often criticised for being empirically insensitive), and in having certain reservations about applying too rigid a perception of power, as presented in, for instance, Lukes' (2005) work on power, the chapter begins by introducing a concept of power with reference to Bourdieu's work on field, capital and doxa (Bourdieu 1991, 2011) and Goffman's work on strategic interaction (Goffman 1970). This combination of scholarly work will ensure an analysis that shows how individuals are shaped by the capacities and resources of the field in which they interact, as well as how they actively create, manipulate and negotiate these resources. As the development of the argument progresses, discussions of agency by, for instance, Hoggett (2001) and Greener (2002) in relation to welfare work will furthermore be introduced.

The introductory chapter explained how Nye's (1990, 2011) concept of soft power has been included in the analysis of welfare encounters in order to analyse the way power works (Haugaard 2003). The goal is to try to 'bridge the power debates', as suggested by Haugaard (2012). He recommends combining the two contrasting views of power: 'one of power as *domination*, largely characterized as *power over*, and the other of power as *empowerment*, frequently theorized as *power* to' (Haugaard 2012: 33 – emphasis in the original). The reason for combining these two traditions is that the type of power at play in encounters between citizens and welfare workers is not best described as hard or constraining. Thus, the power at play in these encounters cannot only be understood from a pluralistic perspective that centres around how conscious actors behave in accordance with expressed interests (the first dimension of power [Dahl 1957]) or emphasises the hidden mechanisms, framings and manipulations of actors' power (the second dimension [Bachrach and Baratz 1962]). Furthermore, the type of power at play in these encounters is not merely about how actors exercise power over other actors. The power at play in welfare encounters also centres around how particular resources and capitals give some actors the (soft) power to define what is taking place, which often has to do with soft issues such as giving and receiving 'help' and 'care'. The encounter between welfare workers and citizens is therefore very much about which persons (agency) and which norms (structure) hold the power to define and frame the expectations of both welfare workers and citizens, which persons and which norms decide what constitutes 'meaningful' help and 'legitimate' actions of both parties (i.e., the third and fourth dimensions of power [Foucault 1983; Lukes 2005]; see also Haugaard's [2012] discussion of this matter).

The reason for using Nye's (1990) concept of soft power is that this concept makes it possible to show how power shapes agendas, attracts and makes others cooperate. Power thus consists of both structural elements and agency. For example, if one were to conduct an analysis of agency in the welfare encounter that positions the (educational) resources of the welfare workers as stronger than those of the citizens, one would then neglect the powerful and currently pervasive ideal of citizens as empowered, co-producers and experts in their own life, an ideal that is especially relevant to the welfare encounter. Therefore, structural elements such as how norms and policies position citizens as experts and how this positioning affects the encounter with the welfare worker are as important to include in the analysis as the agency of the participants. The use of the concept of soft power directs attention to the complex practices of welfare work, which include principles, norms, rationales and ideals, as well as the specific strategies, interests and preferences of the involved individuals. A goal of this present endeavour is thus to remain focused on '*who* is involved in the power relationship (the scope of power) as well as *what* topics are involved (the domain of power)' (Nye 2011: 11 – emphasis in the original).

This somewhat broad definition of soft power has led to a well-known critique: that the concept of soft power is so 'stretched' that the term may come to mean almost everything and therefore almost nothing (Fan 2008: 149), a critique often aimed at Foucauldian studies as well (Haugaard 1997; Lukes 2005). However, this critique is only partially correct, as it implies that in order to conduct a qualified power analysis, one should entirely reject the more discursive or stretched approaches. As Nye (2011: 9) states, there are no tools that allow us to measure power precisely, but power nevertheless has real effects. Or as rightly put by Jenkins,

> In a non-trivial sense, human agency *is* power. Accepting this does not, however, make it easier to understand power: On the one hand, it may simply push the problem to another overloaded word, 'agency' and on the other, the risk of falling into the Foucauldian trap remains. (2013: 147 – emphasis in the original)

These points of criticism emphasise the necessity of remaining pragmatic when analysing power processes. The goal is to avoid getting trapped with the so-called vague Foucauldian concept of power or with the overloaded concept of agency, as suggested by Jenkins (2013). However, the concept of soft power is a reminder of the fact that encounters between welfare workers and citizens may exhibit a much more subtle form of power, and thus perfectly illustrates that power processes are not only about coercion and domination (hard power) (Mik-Meyer and Villadsen 2014). An important differentiation between soft power and the Foucauldian conceptualisation of power (which is also aimed at examining the more subtle nature of power) is, however, that soft power is also agent focused. Soft power is bound to actors such as states, countries and intergovernmental organisations or – in relation to the topic of this book – welfare workers, citizens and welfare organisations and their abilities to set agendas and convince others to cooperate.

Powerful encounters

At its core, power has to do with how individuals, alone or collectively, 'attempt to achieve their objectives and to assist or obstruct others in the achievement of theirs' (Jenkins 2013: 140). In doing so, individuals then deploy different resources meaningful to the contexts in which they (strive to) exercise power. For instance, if a given context is dominated by a rational-legal way of thinking (as in the bureaucracy), then powerful individuals will be those who succeed in activating and employing resources that fit with a rational-legal way of legitimising actions and behaviours. If the context, on the other hand, is dominated by a market rationale, then powerful individuals will be those who succeed in employing resources that fit with a market-oriented way of rationalising. Power can thus be regarded as efficacy, that is, 'how people achieve their ends and fulfil their purposes' (Jenkins 2013: 144). However, one can study neither human agency nor (soft) power per se, as these categories are too broad, too loaded with preconceptions and too open to interpretations. Consequently, the chapters on the bureaucracy (Chapter 5), market (Chapter 6) and psychology (Chapter 7) include discussions of how the participants engage with different rationales and embedded resources, and thus make it possible to study the ways in which soft power works in the encounters between welfare workers and citizens in particular contexts.

A focus on rationales and resources points to the abilities of individuals to achieve particular ends and to the availability of resources within particular contexts. Thus, 'individuals and different groups of actors will have access to differing resources in differing degrees and in differing combinations' (Jenkins 2013: 153). This means that a focus on resources can ensure an analysis of power that equally centres around structural aspects (such as norms, rationales and the availability of resources within particular contexts) and agency (i.e., capability of individuals operating within these contexts). However, when arguing that soft power is related to the dominant rationales and resources of a given context, one must then specify how to define and locate its resources and resourceful individuals, as well as what is actually meant by the concept of context. For this reason, it is important to turn to Bourdieu's analytical concepts of field, social capital, habitus and doxa, as these concepts allow scholars to investigate the rationales and resources of both fields (contexts) and individuals.

Welfare work takes place within organisations that belong to a particular field, for instance, the fields of education, health and care. According to Bourdieu, these fields are all relatively autonomous and each field operates in accordance with a specific rationale or logic that is different from the rationales or logics of the adjacent fields (Bourdieu and Wacquant 1996: 97). However, this is not to imply that all individuals within a field share the views as – or reproduce the same rationale of – the field. The rationale of a field can, in fact, be regarded as a battleground that explicates the power dynamics at play (Emirbayer and Johnson 2008: 6), as newcomers to a field do not (necessarily) share the interests and views of the dominant (and more experienced) players of that field (Bourdieu and Wacquant 1996: 100). The epicentre of this struggle is the availability of a particular social capital for the individual participants. If, for instance, the field of social work operates with a rationale rooted in the importance of the empowered citizen, then there is an implicit demand within this field of citizens to take on an empowered position, voice their situations, share personal and 'honest' experiences and (presumably) be able to present their preferred strategies for solving the particular problem that caused them to engage with the field of social work in the first place (the influences from psychology in welfare work will be further addressed in Chapter 7).

However, many citizens are unable to meet the rationale and demands of, for instance, empowerment because of certain structural elements. It may be that their upbringing and the consequent internalisationn of societis' objective structures have given them a particular habitus that fits badly with the specific rationale of empowerment. In other words, if a citizen is to regard himself or herself as a person who can become – and ought to be – empowered, then he or she has to have a particular habitus. Habitus can thus be regarded as a 'disposition based on a specific stock of knowledge which structures our experience' (Dreher 2016: 63). Habitus gives us access to particular forms of capital, which, in turn, may or may not be useable within a particular field (such as social work). To be a resourceful person within a particular field is therefore a question of possessing a certain kind of habitus or having social capitals that may grant you access to field-specific resources, which then may help you reach the particular and desired end. Social capital is thus simultaneously an aspect of the rationale or logic of a certain field – also sometimes conceptualised as an institutional pattern – and a resource to which individuals have different access (Jenkins 2013: 147–148).

The ideas and rationales that are meaningful within a certain field (e.g., that empowered citizens are preferable to disempowered and passive citizens) are created relationally and according to the dominant perceptions of what kind of behaviour to expect of citizens. Field-specific differences are not rooted in the things themselves but in the dominant structures (norms, rationales, etc.) that govern which actions of individuals may be perceived as meaningful by the dominant actors of the field (Mik-Meyer and Villadsen 2014: 53).

Finally, it is worth mentioning Bourdieu's concept of doxa, as this term refers to the truisms of fields, that is, what constitutes a good or bad argument within a particular field (Mik-Meyer and Villadsen 2014: 55). The truths of a field are often perceived as indisputable by not only the dominant actors of the field but also the dominated actors of the field whom involuntary has been exposed to these truths. The widespread acceptance of the truths (or doxa) within a certain field – for instance, that it is preferred to be an empowered citizen – will therefore ultimately result in a particular type of encounter between citizens and welfare workers. Doxa may thus be regarded as a universal view, which is upheld by dominant political views, public institutions and so forth and may therefore be considered a 'gentle, invisible form of violence' (Bourdieu 2000: 192), or to use the concept of this book, a particular form of soft power. This type of violence or soft power may not be experienced as a practice or act of domination, as actors are also responding to rationales and norm-systems, which are perceived as natural, self-evident and legitimate (Emirbayer and Johnson 2008: 31). A field analysis will therefore begin by locating the principles of division within the specific field in an effort to examine the preconceived and taken-for-granted rationales, which operate within it.

For instance, to divide homeless people into categories such as chronically, transitionally or episodically homeless, as done by social services for the homeless in New York City (Emirbayer and Williams 2005: 706), reveals that homelessness – in this particular context – is a phenomenon organised according to the length of time a person has been in the social work system. However, this study found that the temporal structuring of homelessness (as chronic, transitional or episodic) was saturated with stereotypical perceptions of the homeless person and his or her moral constitution. The encounter between welfare workers and citizens (in this particular case, the homeless) took place in the public sphere but was situated in the intersection between the political field (moral) and the bureaucratic state (principle of organisation). The bureaucratic state and its organizations can thus be regarded as a '"central bank of symbolic power" entrusted with adjudicating disputes over categories and certifying identities' (Wacquant 2013: 276). Hence, there is no doubt that the bureaucracy and its politically motivated organisation of the (social) problems of homeless people have profound and powerful effects on how this kind of welfare work is organised, how homeless people are perceived and, consequently and ultimately, the social lives of the homeless people.

Bourdieu-inspired studies have a strong focus on the structural aspects of domination and power (e.g., the way homelessness is organised) and emphasise the concepts of fields, capital, habitus and doxa (Jenkins 2013; Wacquant 2013; Mik-Meyer and Villadsen 2014). Bourdieu and his followers neither take the motives and agency of individuals as a given nor subscribe to the idea that individuals are able to have genuine strategic intentions (Thévenot 2011: 45). For this reason the work of Goffman will be briefly touched upon, specifically his work that addresses the agency of individuals and their ability to act strategically and calculatively (other parts of his work, which downplay the strategic abilities of individuals, will be included in later chapters). In *Strategic Interaction*, Goffman examines the calculative and gamelike aspects of human interaction. He conceptualises the encounter between individuals as a type of game with fixed rules that apply for all participants but also render certain moves impossible. Although the game metaphor can be interpreted solely with a focus on the restrictions (the rules of the game) of activities, Goffman also explores the many different roles people take upon themselves when encountering others. People may act as the unwitting (i.e., not noticing that other participants interpret their actions), as the naïve (i.e., when participants interpret the actions of others as they appear) and as being in control of the move (i.e., when participants produce acts, which they think will improve their situation) (Goffman 1970: 11–12). Participants' strategic moves may be interpreted as attempts to manipulate the information about themselves when trying to decode the moves of their counterpart. In this sense, Goffman argues, participants try to mislead one another in attempts to win the game and achieve their desired goal. The point here is that there is never a situation in which the participating individuals exclusively depend on what is communicated verbally. Individuals are always spying and being spied on in their interactions with others, as he explains:

> When a respectable motive is given for action, are we to suspect an ulterior one? When an individual supports a promise or a threat with a convincing display of emotional expression, are we to believe him? When an individual seems carried away by feeling, is he intentionally acting this way in order to create an effect? When someone responds to us in a particular way, are we to see this as a spontaneous reaction to the situation or a result of him having canvassed all other possible responses before deciding this one was the most advantageous? (Goffman 1970: 85)

In summary, individuals encounter one another in particular situations (Goffman) or fields (Bourdieu) in which particular social orders or capitals are in place. However, they also continuously spy on each other – and are being spied on – in an effort to achieve whatever outcome they have in mind for the encounter with their fellow participants (agency). It is therefore important that these social conditions for the encounter are brought to the forefront, conditions which become observable when applying the concept of soft power (i.e., the principles, norms, values and ideas of fields, as well as the interests, strategies and preferences of individuals). It is this combination which the concept of soft power captures, that is, how structural aspects (such as norms and rules) and agency affect the welfare encounter and produce particular ways in which welfare workers and citizens can talk about both the goal of the encounter and each other.

When the goal is to understand what goes on in the encounter between welfare workers and citizens, then the particular education and accumulated professional experience of welfare workers are not the most important phenomena to focus on. The ambivalence of structuring an analysis according to concepts such as profession, professional or professionalism is shared in the work of Bourdieu, who paid little attention to the notion of professionalism (Schinkel and Noordegraaf 2011b). In his conversational book with Waquant, Bourdieu explained that he believed 'that one must go further and call into question not only classifications of occupations ... but the very concept of ... *profession*, which has provided the basis for a whole tradition of research ... [which is why one must try] to *replace* this concept with that of field' (Bourdieu and Wacquant 1996: 242 – emphasis in the original).

This critique is aimed especially at the concept of profession itself as it – according to Bourdieu – implies a certain ideological stance that hinders a critical sociological approach to what constitutes a profession or professionalism in the empirical world. For him, a profession is 'essentially a bureaucratic concept that "veils the space of competition and struggle"' (Schinkel and Noordegraaf 2011a: 72–73). Present-day managers and professionals are, however, part of a struggle over symbolic capital that, at its core, concerns what constitutes professional work in a larger field of power. This struggle is, for instance, affected by the recently worsened economic situation of Western countries, which has led to an emphasis on capitals within welfare work that has not been a natural part of this field before (Schinkel and Noordegraaf 2011b: 99). Welfare workers – professionals or otherwise – are part of a specific (welfare) field with certain distributions of economic, cultural and social capitals, as well as a particular kind of taken-for-granted knowledge, the latter of which changes somewhat according to the existing objective reality (such as the worsened economic situation of Western countries).

With inspiration from a Bourdieusian framework, Schinkel and Noordegraff (2011b) examine the battle over (professional) power among welfare workers and managers. These two authors centre their analysis on how the independent fields of management and welfare (and their capitals) relate. Due to the worsened economic situation of many (if not most) welfare states, Schinkel and Noordegraff (2011b: 118) argue that the current struggles over symbolic capital within welfare fields have been infiltrated by managerial aspects, such as NPM and other schemes, which seek to minimise cost and save money. Today's welfare work, whether it concerns assisting jobseekers, homeless people or drug addicts, involves a constant struggle over what it means to act in a professional way – a struggle that can only be defined in relation to the specific field in question. This is why Schinkel and Noordegraaf write extensively about the current de-essentialisation of what it means to be a professional or to be involved in professional work (Schinkel and Noordegraaf 2011a: 93). Social life and its encounters are all about struggles over the legitimate classifications of social problems and people. These struggles are also somewhat arbitrary, as they not only depend on the doxa and capitals of the field in which they take place (Schinkel and Noordegraaf 2011a: 76) but also depend on the individuals who participate in the struggle (e.g., managers) and their capitals as well.

Soft power and agency

The concept of agency is a very central and highly debated concept within sociology, and it would without a doubt be both a very lengthy and somewhat risky undertaking to touch on all the key discussions hereof. Therefore, only the scholarly discussions within social policy research that deal with how agency (and soft power) may be seen as embedded within welfare encounters are in focus here. Citing Williams and Popay (1999), Hoggett argues that social policy research has been organised by a so-called unhelpful dichotomy of blaming either the system or the subject (Hoggett 2001: 37). In research of a more left-wing nature, the blame has typically been placed on the system – 'subject good, society bad' – and efforts have been made to develop accounts of agency that centre the individual participants in the encounter as creative and reflexive (Hoggett 2001: 37). However, even though this positioning of the individual client or patient as resourceful may reflect a positive development within policy research, Hoggett argues for a model of agency able to deal with individuals who also exhibit destructive behaviours towards themselves and others. This model of agency can deal with the negative capacities of the welfare subject and not only measure so-called creative agents against their abilities to act strategically (Hoggett 2001: 38).

Hoggett is sceptical towards the idea of the knowledgeable actor; even when this knowledge is practical and tacit in nature. It all comes down to the question of whether it is 'always true that we know (even tacitly) why we are doing what we are doing when we do it or is a good deal of our reflexivity actually *post hoc?*' (Hoggett 2001: 39). Or put differently, how should the actions or choices of welfare subjects be understood? The main argument of Hogget (2001: 42) is that certain things are just too painful to think about, which is why they rarely become part of an individual's reflections about his or her situation, even when those things may be quite apparent to those around them (bystanders or even researchers). Rather than painful (one might add), things and events may also be so 'natural' for the individual – because they are reproduced in the many settings in which he or she participates – that they likewise become excluded from reflexions and choices.

If citizens act on conscious intent, calculation and impulse, then the model of agency must be able to reflect all these actions. Hoggett makes the convincing argument that clients or patients, for instance, are not only passive and dependent individuals (a perception much previous research has been criticised for having) and therefore advises against wrongly equating agency with constructive coping (Hoggett 2001: 43).

His model of agency is a quadrant model that deals with both non-reflexive and reflexive forms of agency (the vertical axis), as well as self-as-object and self-as-agents (the horizontal axis) (Hoggett 2001: 43, 47). This model thus conceptualises the following four types of agency: (1) reflexive agency, (2) non-reflexive agency, (3) self as non-reflexive object and (4) self as reflexive object. The first quadrant, reflexive agency, implies a responsible agent who acts within a context of constraint. However, this agent is not necessarily a constructively coping agent. This type of agency is the most dynamic form (Greener 2002: 692). The second quadrant, non-reflexive agency, implies a more impulse-driven type of behaviour of agents who (for various reasons) are in a state of, for instance, denial that clouds their ability to be reflexive (or, things and notions that are so 'natural' to the participants that they are simply excluded from their reflexions). This type of agency is also found in Bourdieu's work on the habitual nature of human action (Greener 2002: 694). The quadrant self as non-reflexive object implies agents who have been so dominated by others (well-meaning or otherwise) that they continue to be the object of the work. These individuals also act instinctively but have very little control over their environment (Greener 2002: 696). Finally, the fourth quadrant, the self as reflexive object, implies agents who are able to reflect on the object position given to them – for instance, their marginal position as blacks among Caucasians – and are therefore acutely aware of their own powerlessness (Hoggett 2001: 47–50). This agent is a 'trapped agent', who may be willing to engage with co-participants but is unable to do so because of structural constraints (Greener 2002: 695).

Even though this quadrant model of agency runs the risk of including all actions as expressions of agency and thereby risks weakening the concept altogether (especially the notion of self as non-reflexive object seems to provoke the general understanding of agency), it portrays agency in a more nuanced way than approaches that define agency in terms of the knowledgeable, constructive and/or calculating actor. Hoggett's model of agency neither centres around the capacity of individuals to act in a morally grounded, strategic and calculating manner nor presumes that all individuals know what they want and how to act (strategically) in order to achieve this in, for instance, the welfare encounter. Furthermore, by using the model to analyse the so-called first and second order of agency (Hoggett 2001: 51), he puts even more emphasis on the interactional dimensions of agency. The first order of agency is when changes occur within a pattern i.e., game playing with clear rules, whereas the second order of agency is when citizens and welfare workers challenge the rules of the game. This distinction between the first and second orders of agency makes it possible to investigate how the actions of citizens – who intentionally or unintentionally confront the rules of the game – may alter the ways in which welfare workers can interpret their own work (and thus the rules of the game). Similarly, the notion of the second order of agency may also help to bring different nuances to the foreground in regards to how citizens and welfare workers perceive and interact with each other and how they may attempt to bend or alter the dominant (and sometimes even incompatible) norms and rationales of their encounter. The point here is that both the instinctive and non-reflexive actions of citizens and welfare workers produce the re-actions and hence actions (and consequently agency) of the other party. Therefore, Hoggett argues, it would be problematic to define agency in terms of simply whether the actions of individuals are reflexive:

> We may act involuntarily, against our better judgement. We may act impulsively and bear the cost or enjoy the benefit later. ... To say that actions may have unintended consequences suggests that we had an intention ... but this eludes the point that actions themselves may not be intended. (Hoggett 2001: 52)

This definition of agency is further developed by Greener in his paper 'Agency, Social Theory and Social Policy', in which he explicitly relates Hoggett's four types of agency to the participants' context and to Bourdieu's metaphor of agency as a game (Greener 2002: 702). For instance, those welfare workers who manage payouts for clients based on their evaluation of the client's situation have a particular (economic) capital. Citizens – in the role of receivers of the money – must therefore learn 'to "play" the game of claiming and receiving the best welfare service possible through acquiring knowledge of the system' (Greener 2002: 702). Citizens with a similar habitus to that of the welfare worker will most likely be perceived by the welfare workers as 'one of us' and will consequently receive better service. From this perspective, clients, patients, students and so on are perceived as agents who will try to play the system in an effort to achieve the best possible return (Greener 2002: 702).

According to Greener (2002: 702), a robust policy is consequently one that makes the rules of conduct explicit for all participants. The goal is to reduce the likelihood that the citizens with the 'correct' habitus and capital will receive better treatment than those without these resources who, nevertheless, should receive the same level of (welfare) service. This approach to agency is based on a perception that a person's agency is embedded in particular contexts and social structures, which define them in certain, significant ways.

In a recent paper by Dobson (2015), the author develops this relational approach to agency. Welfare workers and citizens are here assumed to encounter social worlds, which greatly impact the ways in which they construct (and are constructed in) the welfare encounter. When Wright (2012) writes about enacting agency, she – like Dobson (and Goffman) – wishes to emphasise that agency has to do with situated interactions and therefore with the existing power relations within a particular context (Wright 2012: 315) or social world (Goffman 1990b; Dobson 2015). Agency has to do with interconnectedness, interaction and intersubjectivity and is a relational and dynamic concept that can help shed light on a fundamental principle of human interaction, namely, that a person's self cannot be separated from the self of those with whom he or she interacts, which is why agency (with reference to Goffman) must be regarded as 'profoundly enmeshed with shared expectations and accomplished in everyday life through interaction' (Wright 2012: 318).

All this work stipulates that essentialising representations of both organisations and individuals must be abandoned (in this case, the welfare workers and the citizens whom they encounter), as doing so wrongly assumes agency as a property of individual subjects or organisations. Social policy and welfare practice are rather the outcomes of relational and dynamic processes between policy, welfare and the actions of practitioners, a kind of interface expressed through day-to-day actions (Dobson 2015: 688, 692): 'human power and agency are *relationally constitutive of* and *enacted through* institutional space via the study of human power, agency, experience, identity and affect' (Dobson 2015: 695 – emphasis in the original).

The agency of both welfare workers and citizens is, in other words, negotiated in the context of policymaking. This means that the actions of these two parties cannot be regarded as merely the actions of individuals who each operate with their 'own' interests in mind, as if these interests were isolated entities unaffected by the policy context and the other participants in the encounter (Hunter 2003: 332). Even though the professional status of the welfare worker may be important for the encounter with the citizen, one must also bear in mind that welfare workers also hold other social roles and positions with importance for the encounter (Hunter 2003: 333). For this reason, Hunter (2003) suggests the application of a so-called social relations approach to welfare workers in an effort not to wrongly privilege, for instance, the professional background of welfare workers in the analysis of their encounter with citizens. Thus, interaction between the citizen and the welfare worker may actually be influenced by other contextual phenomena, such as common social identifications between the participants or even a particular policy agenda (Hunter 2003: 334).

For instance, in a study on the interactions between users and professionals in a mental health forum, Hodge (2005) found that certain voices were perpetually and consistently excluded from the conversation. The analysis revealed that the agency (and soft power) of the forum users resulted from specific (discursive) interactions which reflected a specific policy agenda (in this case, user involvement initiatives) (Hodge 2005: 165, 177). The dialogue between the mental health professionals and the forum users was policed or steered by a particular policy agenda, which framed the conversations of the forum in a particular way and, according to the author, therefore should be regarded as an expression of (soft) power. Certain issues were effectively kept off the agenda (two-dimensional [2-D] power), and expressions of 'personal experience' by the users were only accepted as relevant if such experiences could be incorporated within the discourse of user involvement, which dominated the forum meetings (3-D and 4-D of power) (Hodge 2005: 177).

Concluding comments

Investigating the soft power of (especially) welfare workers in the encoun-ter with citizens represents a large field of scholarly interest and study. A vast proportion of this research emphasises the institutional selves, that is, the process of a citizen being transformed into a particular type of client or patient in the encounter with the welfare workers (e.g., Gubrium and Holstein 2001; Loseke 2001; Järvinen and Mik-Meyer 2003). The focus within this particular branch of study is predominantly the social construc-tion of clients and patients and how this construction reflects the policy agenda and other organisational phenomena of the particular setting. This focus on how the soft power of especially welfare workers dominates or steers the welfare encounter is not only central to the scholarly field of institutional selves. This focus has moreover become a key point of concern in practice, and several attempts have been made to bring the power of the encounter (back?) into the hands of the welfare recipients and thereby show that citizens too are in possession of agency. The current empha-sis on empowerment and co-production within welfare services reflects this tendency and represents a desire to redistribute the power of welfare encounters in favour of the citizens, who – from this perspective – ought to be given the opportunity to be(come) powerful agents (again).

However, these attempts to empower citizens by placing them in a co-productive relationship with the welfare worker have been heavily criti-cised (see also Chapter 7). In addition to this general critique, the empow-erment movement has also been criticised specifically for including the welfare workers in its mission. It is not only the citizens who ought to be empowered; welfare workers are also expected to be empowered through new and much more engaging policies. The literature responsible for this criticism notes that the aim of empowering welfare workers is to ensure a greater degree of professional discretion within welfare work (which, coincidentally, is also the aim of many de-centralising initiatives). As Peters and Pierre write, the 'empowerment movement argues that organisa-tions will work better if their lower echelons [welfare workers] are given more discretion [and if] clients and citizens ... [are] given greater control over their own lives' (Peters and Pierre 2000: 21). However, this goal of empowering both welfare workers and citizens may – according to these critical authors – result in the de-professionalisation of welfare workers and furthermore only empower citizens who are capable of negotiating with the welfare workers (and thus accepting the capitals of the field). These citizens' request are perceived as 'reasonable' and rational (Peters and Pierre 2000: 24).

There is little doubt that one of the most challenging and powerful aspects of encounters between welfare workers and citizens today is the changes in both the roles of and relationship between these two parties. The relationship between the citizen and the welfare worker is currently being renegotiated according to dominating norms and rationales of how to behave as, respectively, a citizen and a welfare worker. The changing nature of the citizen–welfare worker relationship has furthermore resulted in a series of dilemmas regarding the goal of the welfare work, the roles of the different parties, the construction of legitimacy and (ultimately) responsibility, autonomy and power (Goss 2001: 4). For this reason, Chapter 4 takes a closer look at these and other dilemmas by engaging with the scholarly literature that places the topic of interaction centre-stage.

4

Powerful encounters as seen from an interactionist perspective

Introduction

The sociological literature on the categorisation of citizens in welfare contexts is part of a large field of study. Much of this research is inspired by a symbolic interactionist perspective and examines the dialectical relationship between the actions of individuals and their institutional and organisational contexts.[1] The focus of this work is how individuals respond to the social conditions of which they are part (Hall 1997). However, some scholars argue that public encounters have been given too little attention and that studies such as Lipsky's classic work on street-level bureaucrats and research inspired by him have focused too narrowly on these encounters as inherently problematic (Bartels 2013). For this reason, Bartels (2013: 470) urges researchers to pay more attention to what happens 'in-between' welfare workers and citizens than is currently done, as public encounters are indeed a relational, situated phenomenon.

Although this call for more research that takes a relational approach to the study of welfare encounters is important, it is also crucial to engage with the vast and strong research tradition within micro sociology that explicitly looks at the so-called in-between in welfare work. Much of this research addresses how citizens are categorised by welfare workers in accordance with structural elements such as dominating norms, legislation and notions of the ideal client or patient in various organisational settings (e.g., Valverde 1998; Cruikshank 1999; Holstein and Gubrium 2000; Gubrium and Holstein 2001; Loseke 2001; Miller 2001; Järvinen and Mik-Meyer 2003; Rosenthal and Peccei 2006; Lessenich 2011). Even though some studies have explored how welfare workers and their work are equally influenced and steered by the dominating principles, norms and ideas of the organisation in which they work (for an example hereof, see Järvinen and Mik-Meyer 2012), such research – as well as research that explores how the agency of especially the citizen affects the encounter with welfare workers – is quite rare. There is, in other words, a need for examining the implementation of welfare-to-work policies in organisations, as well as how the current (dominant) goal of making citizens personally responsible for their situations actually modifies the behaviours of citizens and welfare workers (as it leads to new expectations of both encountering parties) (Wright 2012).

The tasks of this chapter are twofold: firstly, to introduce symbolic interactionism, that is, the interactionist approach to studying the in-between as suggested by Bartels (2013), and secondly, to discuss empirical studies of the encounter between welfare workers and citizens, with particular attention to their respective roles, their relationship with one another and the findings of the selected studies. The chapter emphasises the soft power at play between citizens and welfare workers and exemplifies how the structural elements and agency of the two parties frame the encounter. The goal is to present research that shows how both welfare workers and citizens co-produce dominant norms in welfare work and how this (re)production can be perceived as an expression of soft power.

Because the main interest of this book is to investigate how agency relates to structural elements, a key inspiration for this chapter is the symbolic interactionist work by Goffman, as well as more recent research – also inspired by symbolic interactionism – on institutional selves and identity work (see Gubrium and Holstein 2001; Järvinen and Mik-Meyer 2003; Gubrium and Järvinen 2014a). With this scholarly inspiration, it becomes possible to analyse the multiplicity of selves within social policy (e.g., Hoggett 2001).

A symbolic interactionist approach

Symbolic interactionism puts interaction and context in the very centre of the analysis of human actions. The focus of this tradition is both linguistic and bodily actions and their contexts. At the heart of symbolic interactionism lie the practices and actions between people and how these can be regarded as the effects of different ideas and theories within societies and organisations. The identifications of citizens and welfare workers, as well as their perceptions of others, are within an interactionist tradition regarded as products of social processes and are therefore presumed to be created and recreated in social interactions.

Because the interpretations of social actors are believed to have real consequences for the structure of the interaction, a key focus in this line of work is how interacting individuals interpret the particular situation in which they are part and how this structures their interactions. The individual person is expected to structure different roles, which are related to the social order of the encounter (Goffman 1990b). A change of footing – the way in which the individual positions himself or herself – is affected by micro actions, including non-verbal expressions of fellow participants. For instance, a shift in tone or 'a strip of behaviour that is less long than a grammatical sentence' can have profound effects on the encounter and its outcome (Goffman 1981: 128). Goffman is interested in the situated activity; how identities and identification processes are negotiated in practice. He pays particular attention to relational meaning (the so-called in-between) and therefore emphasises what people say and do and how their physical and linguistic statements relate to the situation in which these actions take place (Goffman 1967, 1974, 1990b).

In Goffman-inspired research, there is a plethora of studies that investigate how individual actors juggle a variety of roles and often conflicting descriptions of the researched phenomenon. This particular branch of research assumes that everyday (organisational) life is filled with contradictory actions. These actions arae produced and reproduced by a social order (or a definition of situation), which consequently becomes the focal point of the analysis (Goffman 1990b). According to Manning (2000: 288), the main project of Goffman was in this way to develop a theory of credibility: 'he analyzed the ways in which people make their performances convincingly real', which is why his work can be regarded as essentially about researching the social conditions that make particular actions of individuals credible in one situation but not in others.

The emphasis on the social conditions for the encounter between welfare workers and citizens points to an important aspect of the analysis, namely, that these two parties can only define themselves in accordance with statuses, roles and relationships that are consistent with the social order of the situation (Mik-Meyer and Villadsen 2014). Or put differently, if a citizen perceives the welfare worker assigned to his or her case as someone who ought to deliver a service to him or her, then this expectation or social order affects the roles available to the welfare worker (i.e., as someone whose main task is to deliver a service), as well as the roles available to the citizen (i.e., as someone who may expect to be serviced). These expectations are related to policies and norms of society, which – by definition – are changeable and not fixed entities. This means that the welfare context and social order of, for instance, employment services will automatically vary over time and in relation to the perception of unemployment as, for instance, related to structural problems of the labour market or individual problems of the unemployed. Accordingly, welfare workers' and citizens' identifications and perceptions of each other will automatically vary in accordance with the dominant perception of unemployment.

The concept of social order (of unemployment) reveals that encounters between welfare workers and citizens are not random and unpredictable but rather relate to the participants' expectations of the meeting (e.g., how to resolve the problem of unemployment), which, in turn, are anchored in structural elements, such as policy, legislation and dominating ideas of how citizens and welfare workers ought to behave.

The agency of welfare workers and citizens can be investigated as (possibly successful) attempts to make their definition of the situation, that is, their perception of what the encounter should be about, the winning definition. However, this may not always be possible, which is why the participants may have to adjust their behaviour to a definition of the situation that does not align with their preferred definition. In Goffman's terms, both cases will require participants to perform face work: they will adjust their faces so they correspond to the winning definition of the situation in which they participate (Goffman 1990b). In order for an interaction to be nonconflictual, it is therefore essential that participants agree on what kind of situation they engage in. For instance, is it a situation about getting a job, talking about personal problems or a third matter? Should the citizen expect service, legal advice or coaching from the welfare worker and, conversely, should the welfare worker expect the citizen to want to be serviced, receive legal advice or be coached? However, sometimes it is not possible for the participants of an encounter to reach an agreement on how the given situation must be understood, and in such cases the participants compete in an effort to make their definition of the situation the defining one. If they fail to do so, they will then adjust their actions to the winning definition. From a power perspective, it is therefore important to recognise the two following points: firstly, that the participants of an encounter are continuously aware of each other, and secondly, that their (respective) understandings and interpretations are embedded within the existing social order and its dominant norms and rationales.

Institutional selves and agency

When using the concept of institutional selves, the authors within this scholarly work continue to draw on symbolic interactionism and specifically on a field of study within sociology that investigates how welfare workers' perceptions of the citizens they encounter actually reflect the ways in which the work is organised, their respective professional approaches, the legislation of the particular welfare area and other structural aspects of the work (see, e.g., Holstein and Gubrium 2000; Gubrium and Holstein 2001; Gubrium and Järvinen 2014a). Some of the more classic studies look at organisations which help people who are victims of abuse (Loseke 1989,

1992), unemployed, in therapy (Miller 1992), old and live in care facilities (Gubrium 1986) and so on. The common goal of these studies is not primarily to achieve a more nuanced, deeper and better understanding of the particular citizen groups and their problems or to regard either one as detached from the organisational context. Their aim is rather to achieve a better understanding of how organisational aspects frame the encounter between the staff working in these organisations and the citizen, aspects which make particular kinds of selves possible.

In the introductory chapter of *Institutional Selves* (2001), Gubrium and Holstein propose a distinction between an everyday folk psychology understanding of the self as a discrete, private entity and a postmodern self (an understanding they themselves subscribe to) defined by the social contexts of people's lives (Gubrium and Holstein 2001: 2). The authors draw on the work of Hochschild (1983) and others in conceptualising the prevalent everyday folk psychology understanding of identity as a fundamentally personal construct. Within this conceptualisation, the self is perceived as battling and fighting against a world external to it. The strength of the self is presumed to stem from its '*interiority*; a characteristic described by metaphors such as "*volume*" and "*depth*"' (Gubrium and Holstein 2001: 4 – emphasis in the original). A postmodern self is – as opposed to this psychological self – essentially a social structure and unfolds 'within society, never in some private space separate from it' (Gubrium and Holstein 2001: 6).

The explicit focus here is how the practices of welfare organisations relate to the many highly specialised and quickly expanding organisations within postmodern society. Because the main goal of these organisations is to define and resolve the personal problems of citizens, they become part of the so-called troubled-persons industry (Loseke 1999: 165). The important task for these scholars is consequently to shed light on the identity work in which organisational aspects are transformed into personal qualities, for instance, how the choice of a certain type of therapy makes way for certain narratives about a person (Miller 2001: 81), a so-called *claim-making* activity (Spector and Kitsuse 2001). This concept of claim-making indicates a process in which claims about the problem of a citizen, as well as its causes and solutions, are created – in other words, that social problems are not expressions of objective conditions (Spector and Kitsuse 2001: x). A social problem is rather the result of a process of definition, that is, an activity in which different interacting actors reach an agreement on what to perceive and define as desirable and undesirable social states (Spector and Kitsuse 2001: xi).

More recent research has also brought the processes of defining the problems of citizens to the forefront. One study shows how a dominant rationality of choice both transforms current drug treatment practices and constructs drug-addicted citizens as 'active consumers of welfare services and free and self-managing individuals' (Bjerge *et al.* 2014: 59). On a similar note, another study within the same scholarly field has revealed a clash between two perceptions of drug users: victims of wider social issues or self-responsible actors (Moore 2009). In the latter case, the study revealed that the drug users' own descriptions were consistent with neoliberal principles and discourses, as they placed great importance on self-reliance and independence in their answers. However, the welfare workers described the drug users in accordance with descriptions found in policy reports and referred to them as '"drug dependents", "vulnerable", "marginalised", "hard-to-reach", having "complex needs" or "at-risk"' (Moore 2009: 1163), while paradoxically – and simultaneously – offering welfare services which placed the drug users in a position of the responsible subject. In order to understand what goes on in the encounter between drug users and welfare workers, there are quite a number of contexts which the researcher must be aware of, contexts that can explain the (sometimes conflicting) interactions between the two parties by highlighting the different situational definitions (e.g., are welfare workers supposed to treat or coach?), as well as the differing perceptions of the drug users (e.g., are they to be perceived as vulnerable clients or independent actors?) and their problems (e.g., do they have medical or psychosocial problems?).

It is easy to assume that the perception of citizens within welfare work – as someone who should be helped, serviced and empowered – is anchored in the routines of the work, the legislation regulating the particular welfare area, the ways in which the particular welfare work is organised and so on. However, perceptions of citizens not only reflect a local organisational reality; they also reflect societal tendencies of how to conduct professional welfare work, as illustrated in policy reports (as in the example of drug users), societal debates and so on. They may even reflect more general structural features, which simultaneously define the welfare work (such as the asymmetry between welfare workers and citizens). Institutional selves is therefore a concept that not only applies to work conducted within physical organisations or workplaces. Welfare encounters, which take place in the streets among street workers and homeless people or drug addicts, for instance, are also affected by market principles and norms from psychology of how to perceive the problems (and identities) of people in need of help (as illustrated in the example of drug users). The concept of institutional selves thus reflects both ideas integrated in (physical) organisations where the encounter takes place and more general ideas in society about the troubles at hand.

When welfare workers turn 'troubles into problems' (e.g., smoking hash or being addicted to drugs) and thus transform whatever issues the citizens are facing into psychological, medical or legal problems, they in addition create serviceable problems (Gubrium and Järvinen 2014b: 1). While *troubles* is a rather vague term, the idea of serviceable problems is, on the other hand, characterised by apparent clarity (Gubrium and Järvinen 2014b: 3). This clarity is a result of the self-evidence of the institutionalised social problems of citizens; what is perceived as 'clear and evident becomes virtually unnoticed and, by virtue of that, "unremarkable"' (Brekhus [1998] quoted in Gubrium and Järvinen 2014b: 4). Furthermore, this transformation process of turning troubles into problems relates to policy and consequently has to do with what at a given time in history can be serviced or handled in the everyday encounter between welfare workers and citizens (Järvinen and Mik-Meyer 2003; Gubrium and Järvinen 2014b: 1). However, research that centres around the powerful transformation of citizens' troubles into recognisable social problems (Davis 1988) or investigates the impact of policy, legislation and so forth on the availability of professional identifications for welfare workers (e.g., Lipsky 2010; Järvinen and Mik-Meyer 2012) tends to downplay how the expectations of citizens regarding the actions and behaviours of welfare workers affect the welfare encounter. Citizens may, for instance, expect welfare workers to provide service or coaching, which in turn will affect (and limit) the ways in which the welfare encounter may unfold. It is not just welfare workers who categorise and label citizens in the encounter, as citizens also enter these meetings with particular expectations and ways of framing their troubles (Davis 1988). For instance, in Davis' (1988) conversation-analytical examination of the interactions between male doctors and female patients, she found that a so-called 'friendship frame' was a powerful context for this encounter. However, her study also revealed that the expectations of the female patients were equally powerful for the encounter. It is, in other words, not only the male GPs, the bureaucratic principles and the medical norms which govern the encounter; the female patients' own expectations played a powerful role in the encounter as well.

The next three chapters will consequently illustrate how certain expectations of how to conduct legitimate welfare work are expressed by both welfare workers and citizens. These expectations are immensely powerful (especially when shared), as they frame the encounter between the citizens and the welfare workers in a certain obvious way for all participants. It may, in other words, not only be citizens who are subjected to a clientisation process (Gubrium and Järvinen 2014b), as welfare workers may similarly find themselves in a dependency relation formed by the powerful expectations of how to engage in legitimate relations in today's welfare organisations. Both citizens and welfare workers are equipped with institutional selves, and the agency of these two parties is affected by this particular positioning. Because these institutional selves reflect norm-based expectations of how to behave as a citizen (in need of help, service, etc.) and welfare worker (to provide help, service, etc.), they are quite powerful, as they set the rules for what may be understood as meaningful interactions in the welfare encounter. It is therefore the 'directing, conditioning and shaping influences of social organization' (Hall 1997: 397) that is in focus within this branch of sociological research. The social organisation and dominant perceptions are so much more than passive contexts or merely the background for the encounters between welfare workers and citizens.

Consequently, Hall suggests to engage in meso-domain analyses in an effort to analyse the so-called meta-powers at play in the encounter. Hall's concept of meta-power is somewhat similar to Bachrach and Baratz's (1962) classic and influential work 'Two Faces of Power', in which they discuss how dominant values, procedures and rules mobilise a particular type of bias in human interaction, that benefits the power and actions of certain individuals. The concept of meta-power is also somewhat inspired by the third face of power, namely, that the exercise of power also concerns the manipulation of individual consciousness, that policy agents have a particular type of knowledge from which they can never escape and which forms and inspires their actions (Lukes 2005). These are the understandings which Hall's (1997: 398) concepts of meso-domain and meta-power relate to: that analyses of encounters between individuals always connect to – what he calls – a larger environment which exists beyond the observed situated activity. In the micro analyses conducted by scholars such as Goffman and his followers, there is a strong focus on how the conditionality of the interaction shapes the actions of the participants. Thus, this type of analysis does not typically address the larger environment outside the observed activity, which is perhaps why Goffman himself never wrote explicitly about power, even though, as Jenkins (2008) and Mik-Meyer and Villadsen (2014) have pointed out, most of his work can indeed be seen as demonstrations of power in encounters between individuals. Hall (1997), however, seeks to address this overlooked and under-researched issue of how structural aspects (policy, legislation, economy, principles, norms, etc.) which may not be visible in the studied interaction but nevertheless greatly impact the investigated encounter:

> Meta-power involves altering or creating conditions and situations and providing the grounds and tools for delegates, often by explicit decision-making and other actions. It is a pervasive, substantial, and critical (but under-examined) form of power. While it involves defining situations, it is more than that due to the active construction and organization of situations. (Hall 1997: 415)

When investigating what goes on in encounters between individuals, Hall (1997: 401) argues that one should not only consider what goes on within a given situation (an analysis of first-order agency), as many interactionists do. Instead, he argues that one must also take a so-called meta-power approach (an analysis of second-order agency) and explore how the social organisation of a situation relates to the structural phenomena beyond it. The goal of a meso-domain analysis is, thus, to investigate how the social organisation of interactions between individuals is the product of the actions and behaviours of the participants, as well as the structures and history of the investigated field.

Hall (1997) uses his own research within the field of education to exemplify how, for instance, policy agents depend on other individuals in order to carry out their intensions. The actions of policy agents can be seen as constructed by their knowledge of how their decisions will affect other actors in the future (Hall 1997: 401). The social organisations of particular situations must therefore be perceived as 'multilevel, complex networks of social sites and relationships that extend across space and time', as he writes (Hall 1997: 414).

It is, of course, not only policy agents whose actions are affected by their awareness that their work affects the work (lives) of both welfare workers and citizens. Welfare workers – the street-level staff – are also influenced by policy agendas and are also (presumably) aware that their actions and decisions can have large impacts for the citizens they are encountering. Similarly, the actions of citizens must in addition be seen as reflecting both the agenda of the particular encounter and their own interpretations of how their actions may either strengthen or weaken the possibility of them achieving what they want from the welfare encounter. The importance of individuals' intentions in Hall's (1997) concept of meta-power should, therefore, be added to the ways in which soft power is used here: the agenda of a society (e.g., its policy agenda) is automatically embedded within the agendas of organisations and specific situations, whether the participants are aware of this or not. As argued by Haugaard (2003, 2012), power in complex societies is predominantly based on the reproduction of a shared perception of actors that enables them to act together in ways in which they would otherwise never do. It is this dual focus on agency and structure captured in the concept of soft power – an ambition to 'provide conceptual space for a large number of aspects of the creation of power which, to date, have been theorized in incommensurable paradigms' (Haugaard 2003: 87) – that gives this concept its strengths: agents have intentions and engage in explicitly asymmetrical relations in which they try to act strategically, but they are simultaneously individuals who encounter co-participants in concrete situations influenced by societal and organisational agendas, which they may not be aware of but by which they are nevertheless affected as a consequence of the awareness of their co-participants.

For instance, when a school principal in her interactions with her faculty revealed a 'deeply ingrained cultural style' that rested on commanding, goal orientation, adherence to rules, respect and so forth (Hallett 2007: 156), the teachers rejected this type of leadership, as for them, this behaviour corresponded neither with the social order of the school nor with how – in their minds – a principal should engage with the faculty. However, the authoritative style of the principal did result in respect from the local school council, where her emphasis on goal orientation and adherence to rules was very well received (Hallett 2007: 167). This finding shows the importance of investigating how a situated activity is related to 'complex networks of social sites and relationships that extend across space and time' (Hall 1997: 414), in this case, the behaviour of a school principal that is saturated with goal orientations and adherence to rules as stipulated in policy agendas. The findings also illustrate that powerful individuals – those whose interpretation of the situation becomes the dominant view – are individuals with a 'breath of perspective ... [and therefore] control' (Hall 1997: 398), who as a result know how to act in meaningful ways (in this example, in faculty meetings and in meetings with the local school council) and who are flexible in adjusting their behaviour to the situated activities in which they take part. To be powerful is thus to be able to use one's (different) capitals in encounters as they give 'the *power to define the situation* in which the interactions that comprise the negotiated order takes place' (Hallett 2003: 133 – emphasis in the original). What makes these actors powerful is their capacity to play according to the appropriate rules of each field. Such actors hold multiple types of social capital, each one of them appropriate to the respective field in which they play.

Another study that combines an interactionist approach to (in this case, doctor–patient) encounters with Bourdieu's theory of practice is that of Stokes and colleagues (2006: 632), who examine the 'micro-macro link' between the actions of individuals and the capitals within the powerful field of health. This approach results in the analysis of the forms of capital and symbolic power at play in situations of rule breaching in doctor–patient encounters. The researchers found that when (micro) rules were broken, then both parties were suddenly acutely aware of the distributions of power in the encounter (Stokes *et al.* 2006: 617). By analysing the breaking of rules, the authors illustrate the different capitals at play, capitals which were used to define the situation and to uphold the ceremonial order

between the two parties (Stokes *et al.* 2006: 631). Yet another study of the
field of health similarly explores how nurses' stories of doctors rhetorically
draw on the public debates and disputes about nursing and medicine in
general (Allen 2001). In this study, the researcher shows how contemporary debates in society are brought by the nurses into their work in an effort
for them to justify or solidify their arguments and claims about their occupational group and the norm of their profession (Allen 2001).

Public debates and disputes about nursing and medicine are one example
of how a larger environment (Hall 1997) can affect an encounter. The larger
environment can, however, also be expressed in terms of more classic sociological factors, such as race or social class. For instance, a US study revealed
how Caucasians consistently had more positive and informative interactions
with welfare workers than any other race or ethnic group. In this case, African
Americans, Asian Americans and American Latinnos experienced a much
larger degree of 'rude or dismissive behavior' such as 'raised voices, aggres-
sive body language, combined with a refusal of staff to answer questions or
purposely withhold information', as well as 'impatient or hurried interactions'
(Ernst *et al.* 2013: 1295). Similarly, a German study shows how encounters
between unemployed citizens and welfare workers differ according to the
social class of the participants. Not only does social class shape the ways in
which the welfare workers interact with the citizens; it also shapes the ways in
which the citizens interact with employment services and their staff:

> Unemployed people with a professional background are more likely to look
> down on the 'incompetent' administration. ... Lower-class clients ... approach
> the administration with mixed feelings of fear and hope, which amount to
> [them] 'looking up' to the administration. ... Middle-class clients ... try to meet
> the staff on an equal footing, especially given that their caseworkers have
> similar qualifications to their own and that they have an affinity for adminis-
> trative procedures. (Ludwig-Mayerhofer *et al.* 2014: 670)

Ludwig-Mayerhofer and colleagues (2014) conclude that there are great
differences in agency among unemployed citizens within the public employment services in Germany, a difference that to a large degree is attributed to
the social class of the unemployed citizen (Ludwig-Mayerhofer *et al.* 2014:
608). Hoggett's (2001) first and second order of agency make it possible
to show how the unemployed citizens from lower social classes are only
able to take on the first order of agency, whereas unemployed people from
higher social classes are able to take on the second order of agency as well
(negatively evaluating not only their encounter with the welfare worker
[first order] but the whole administration, which for them appears utterly
incompetent [second order]).

The agency of citizens in this particular study thus relates directly to their social class. However, when considering the agency of welfare workers, their ability to engage in the first or second order of agency may also be related to their 'vulnerability to policy change', as found by another study. In this particular study, the researchers showed how the vulnerability to policy change corresponded with the length of the welfare workers' educational background, as professions with shorter educational backgrounds appeared as more vulnerable to changes in policy (Hall *et al.* 2010: 348). Hall and colleagues (2010: 349) found that semi-professionals (teachers, social workers, nurses, etc.) were more vulnerable to changes in policies and therefore had to do more 'boundary work' than professions with long educations (who hold a solidified expert position) and were better able to apply second-order agency.

In summary, whether the welfare workers are professionals, semi-professionals or workers without any educational training for conducting the welfare work, there is no doubt that the larger environment (be it public debates on policy areas, professional norms, ethicity, social class, lenght of education, gender, new ways of discussing citizens, etc.) affects the welfare encounter. Even if the effects of the larger environment may not be observable when analysing a single welfare encounter, the larger environment will become observable when investigating many encounters and even more observable when relating the findings of these investigations to other sociological studies on the same studied phenomena. The next three chapters will take a closer look at three sets of principles and norm-systems which affect the encounter between citizens and welfare workers.

Note

1. The terms *social order, definition of situation* and *social condition* will be used interchangeably to describe this context.

Part II

The bureaucratic, market and psychology-inspired contexts

5

The bureaucratic context: administrator–client

Introduction

Most welfare work takes place in organisations which resemble or have traits from bureaucracies. The principles and norms of bureaucracies are an important context for welfare work and have therefore resulted in the production of a great amount of scholarly work by political scientists and sociologists on how bureaucratic rules, procedures and principles affect the encounter between welfare workers and citizens.[1] A dominant approach within this literature is to examine how welfare workers resolve the ambiguities of their work conditions, or how they follow rules and routines when dealing with the complex social problems of citizens. Therefore, this branch of research most often centres around the discretionary practices of welfare workers, for instance, how they solve the problem of implementing rules on concrete cases. Accordingly, this chapter also pays special attention to discretionary practices when discussing how the bureaucratic context affects the encounter between welfare workers and citizens.

The primary focus of the chapter is not the organisation of bureaucracies; it is rather the (stronger or weaker) effects of bureaucratic rules, procedures, values and so forth in encounters between welfare workers and citizens in bureaucratic organisations (Hall 1963). The chapter begins with a brief introduction to Weber's definition of the ideal-type bureaucracy, after which the work of Lipsky (2010) and Lipsky-inspired scholars on the discretionary practices of street-level bureaucrats is introduced (e.g., Evans and Harris 2004; Hupe and Hill 2007; Ellis 2011). In the last section, this discussion of discretionary practices is expanded on by investigating the role of agency in this work and by introducing Maynard-Moody and Musheno's (2000, 2003, 2012) concepts of state agents and citizen agents in bureaucratic settings, as well as Dubois' (2010) analysis of (welfare) agents as actors who hold two bodies.

A very short definition of bureaucracy

On a general level, bureaucracy can be described as an organisational form characterised by a division of labour based on functional specialisations that produces a system of procedures for dealing with particular work situations. Hierarchical structures and clear lines of authority define this type of organisation. Experts and staff adhere to routines and extensive rules while being compliant and loyal to the organisation and impartial to their clients (Weber 2013). A characteristic principle of bureaucracy is 'the abstract regularity of the exercise of authority, which is a result of the demand for "equality before the law" ... [and] the principled rejection of doing business "from case to case"' (Weber 2013: 983).

Even though Weber (2013: 991) argues that whether the power of bureaucracies is increasing (or not) in modern states is an empirical question, he still considered – at the time of writing – the bureaucratic organisation to be the most technically developed 'power instrument in the hands of its controller'. According to him, the trained official of the ideal-type bureaucracy will always be superior to the public (i.e., the users of the bureaucratic administration), not least because the bureaucratic administration tends to hide its knowledge (Weber 2013: 991–992). Modern public organisations undoubtedly show some resemblance to this Weberian bureaucracy, and there is no doubt that the bureaucracy, in some aspects, can be seen as a technically superior type of organisation compared with other organisational forms, especially because of the bureaucracy's 'precision, speed, unambiguity, knowledge of the files, continuity, discretion, unity, strict subordination' (Weber 2013: 973). For instance, social workers 'operate under well-defined rules and procedures ... [they] complete enormous amounts of paperwork tracking their cases', and at the same time, it is almost impossible for them to reduce their levels of discretion (Brehm and Gates 1997: 110).

In other words, Weber's bureaucracy with its rational-legal authority, well-defined assignments and rule-bound functions of bureaucrats is perhaps an ideal type even more so today than ever before (du Gay 2000). The concept of bureaucracy is a theoretical construct that must not be seen as a mirror of the real world and its practices. In fact, the ideal-type bureaucracy differs quite a bit from modern bureaucracies. Several other empirical studies have shown that the efficient and rational-legal way of organising human behaviour within this type of organisation, 'the abstract regularity of the exercise of authority ... [and the] rejection of doing business "from case to case"' (Weber 2013: 983), shows very little resemblance to what is actually going on in a number of bureaucratic settings in which staff and citizens meet. This is perhaps most famously demonstrated in Lipsky's (2010) classic study *Street-Level Bureaucracy*. In this study, Lipsky examines – among other things – how much staff discretion can be seen as caused by the goal ambiguity of many public bureaucracies, which aim to help or treat various groups of citizens. The limitations of the bureaucratic model have caused some scholars to put forth the suggestion of perceiving public organisations as units with stronger or weaker resemblances to the Weberian ideal-type bureaucracy, that is, to define bureaucracies in terms of degree rather than kind (Hall 1963: 37). Their argument is that bureaucratic settings cover a range of very different practices, which may have stronger or weaker ties to the classic dimensions of bureaucracies, for instance, hierarchy of author-ity, division of labour, rules, procedures, principles of impersonality and technical qualifications (Hall 1963: 38). The rest of the chapter focuses on key studies within the scholarly literature on the bureaucracy, studies which highlight the bureaucratic features of client–staff encounters, but do so with emphasis on how especially the welfare staff tries to overcome the (bureaucratic) obstacles by engaging in discretionary practices.

Discretionary assessments in bureaucracies

Lipsky's *Street-Level Bureaucracy*, first published in 1980, has to this day great influence on research on the encounter between Lipsky's street-level bureaucrats – here, welfare workers – and citizens. His engagement with the work conditions of front-line staff working in bureaucratic organisations examined from a bottom-up perspective has stimulated much academic work, as these conditions do not produce 'straightforward encounters' (Lipsky 2010: xi). Staff working in these organisations typically have a massive caseload alongside ambiguous and inherently contradictory organisational goals for their work. This means that they have to exer-cise considerable amounts of discretion when applying rules to concrete cases (Wagenaar 2004: 651) in the day-to-day implementation of policy programmes, even though they are supposed to (only) follow the rules and routines of the bureaucracy. According to Lipsky, idealists (i.e., the very dedicated staff) are therefore least suited for employment in bureaucratic organisations. The ideal employees in this type of organisation are rather individuals who are unfazed by the discrepancies between what they are supposed to do and what they actually end up doing (Lipsky 2010: 143). In other words, they are individuals who embody the unengaged, impartial and neutral official of the ideal-type bureaucracy.

The goal of helping citizens on the basis of individual cases often contra-dicts the administrative rules and structures of bureaucratic organisa-tions. In order to analyse the dynamics of discretionary practices (and not just how policy designs are thought out), Lipsky's bottom-up perspective favours empirical investigations of actual practices in this type of organisation. His approach thus encourages the analysis *of* policymaking and not just analysis *for* policymaking (Spicker 2006: v), which until the 1970s was the dominant way of engaging with this area of research (Ellis 2011: 222).

There are two critical dimensions in relation to encounters within organisations highly influenced by bureaucratic principles. Firstly, staff in these organisations have to exercise discretion, which means that they cannot do their jobs according to the highest standard of decision-making, often due to a lack of time, information or other resources necessary in order to respond properly to the individual case. For this reason, they develop routines of practices and simplify their clientele and environment in ways which affect the encounter and hence the outcome of the encounter (Lipsky 2010: xi–xii). Secondly, the work of staff in bureaucratic organisations entails an essential paradox: their work is typically scripted to obtain certain policy objectives; however, the work also demands that they – whether a teacher, a social worker or a judge – simultaneously improvise and remain sensitive to the individual case. According to Lipsky (2010: xii), the title of his book points to this paradox: 'Bureaucracy implies a set of rules and structures of authority, street-level implies a distance from the center where authority presumably resides'. Or put differently, staff in this type of organisation must treat all citizens with similar claims alike (policy as written), but they must moreover respond to the individual citizen's case (policy as performed) (Lipsky 2010: xvii).

Lipsky's discussion of discretionary practices has been criticised for corresponding only with a bureau-professional regime (Clarke *et al.* 1994: 22–23); that is, the practices in this type of organisation are first and foremost controlled by bureaucratic standards, rules and principles. According to Ellis (2011), this means that Lipsky's concept of discretion (only) centres around administrative discretion and not, for instance, norm discretion, which is not linked to the bureaucracy but is achieved through professional training and code of conduct (Ellis 2011: 223) or (as the next two chapters will show) stems from values of the market (Chapter 6) and norms from psychology (Chapter 7).

However, even though this criticism pinpoints a weakness in Lipsky's work it will not be furter elaborated here. Instead some of the central findings of his work will be discussed. They can be summarised by the following five points: (1) resources are most often inadequate to the work task; (2) there is a high service demand; (3) goals are ambiguous, vague or conflicting; (4) it is difficult to measure whether goals are met (because of their conflicting nature); and (5) the presence of clients is involuntary (Lipsky 2010: 27–28). Resources and service are without doubt important factors to include in an analysis of welfare encounters. Nevertheless, the focus here is on the ambiguous goals of the bureaucracy and hence the difficulties in measuring whether they are met (the aforementioned points 3 and 4), as well as the presence of involuntary clients (the aforementioned point 5). Ambiguous goals and involuntary clients are conditions which create a particular and important context for the welfare encounter, especially when investigating the roles and positions available to welfare staff and citizens.

Ambiguous and conflicting goals

Most of the welfare issues (especially within the area of social work) which result in encounters between welfare workers and citizens are complex and consequently hard to define in any clear-cut way. The goals of the work – how to solve the social problems of citizens – may be unclear or contradictory for many reasons, not least because there are changing conceptions of how to solve particular types of problems in society (Lipsky 2010: 165). Staff in organisations influenced by bureaucratic principles encounter, for instance, students who need to perform better, unemployed citizens who need to earn a living and addicts who need help to overcome their substance abuse. In other words, the targeted problems of welfare areas as diverse as education, employment and addiction are complex and will automatically be addressed in a number of different ways. For instance, and related to the previously mentioned examples, is the student's inadequate performance related to psychological stress (which can be caused by a number of things), dyslexia or a problematic relationship with his or her teacher or parents? Is the unemployed person without a job because of a lack of technical or psychological skills, laziness or the structure of the labour market? Do the causes for substance abuse and addiction relate to psychological or social factors? As the list suggests, there are many possible ways of transforming troubles into explicable social problems (Gubrium and Järvinen 2014b). However, staff's choice of (bureaucratic) explanatory models greatly affects their clients, as their perception will result in the implementation of certain procedures and rules rather than of others. The uncertainties of the work also relate to other complexities, for instance, that the definition of the social problem of a citizen is often vague, unclear and contested. The person experiencing the problem may have one way of perceiving the problem and its solution, the welfare staff another and the bureaucratic organisation a third (Lipsky 2010: 41).

What is central here is that the welfare issues are no less complex just because they are dealt with in a rule-abiding type of organisation. Often, the situations of citizens are too complex to be reduced to programmatic formats, which is why staff cannot only adhere to the principles and rules of bureaucracies in order to actually solve the problems, but have to develop discretionary practices rooted in their prior experiences with the particular kind of problem at hand. Consequently, staff make discretionary judgements based on rules and/or stereotypical perceptions of the citizen's problem, which is, a simplification of the complex phenomenon that characterises the citizen's situation and which is often both prejudicial and inaccurate but is nevertheless regarded as better than blindly following the rules, procedures and programmes of the organisation (Lipsky 2010: 142). What is demanded of the staff in bureaucratic organisations is to be compassionate and flexible on the one hand and impartial and rigidly rule adhering on the other (Lipsky 2010: 15–16).

This dual role of acting as both a helper and a controller gives welfare workers in these organisations a very unique position: they get to decide whether the client is truthful, credible and competent, which gives them a type of power that is in conflict with their other roles as service providers or (the more neutral role of) administrators (Lipsky 2010: 61, 74). In order for them to ease their work, they have to obtain and ensure client compliance, as to encourage the clients to voice their opinions will create other problems for the staff, as they then will have to work with (even more) uncontrollable issues (Lipsky 2010: 82, 101). This ambiguity leads to a so-called creaming of clients, that is, preferring clients who are likely to succeed in accordance with the rules and procedures of the organisation and thereby optimise the staff's own performance (Lipsky 2010: 107–108). Another challenge to the highly valued impartiality principle of the bureaucratic organisation is that some clients may appear sympathetic while others are more hostile towards the staff, which, in turn, impacts and biases the evaluation of the client and his or her situation (Lipsky 2010: 108). This problem of bias is quite important in bureaucratic organisations, as it challenges the legitimacy of government and thereby the perception of what it takes for an organisation to be perceived as bureaucratically functioning and legitimate (Lipsky 2010: 116).

As these many examples show, the social order of the bureaucratic encounter appears to be saturated with ambiguities, perhaps most importantly that staff in bureaucratic organisations are expected to follow the rules and procedures of their organisation while being flexible towards the problem situation of the individual citizen they encounter. This embedded ambiguity in the bureaucratic encounter may eventually lead to conflicts between the staff and the citizen, as it must be expected that the two parties will not always agree on when it is appropriate to follow rules and when to be flexible.

Involuntary clients

Another important feature of the bureaucratic organisation is the fact that the presence of clients is (more often than not) involuntary. In the US setting, as investigated by Lipsky, most citizens encounter the bureaucratic organisation involuntarily. In many cases this circumstance is also transferable to welfare states in which a universalistic welfare model is dominant (Järvinen and Mik-Meyer 2003, 2012). For Lipsky, involuntarity of clients leads to an asymmetry between the welfare worker and the citizen: 'to designate or treat someone as a welfare recipient, a juvenile delinquent etc., affects the relationships to that person and also affects the person's self-evaluation' (Lipsky 2010: 9). When Lipsky emphasises that clients and other welfare recipients are in an involuntary position, it is because he then argues that the staff in bureaucratic organisations cannot be disciplined by the clients. The disciplining aspect of the work is, according to him, unidirectional.

The welfare worker must of course manage any complaints of clients, but they are not obliged to change or alter policies in response to dissatisfied clients as service providers must do when faced with dissatisfied customers (Lipsky 2010: 55). Rather, staff in bureaucratic organisations may teach the clients to behave 'properly' and may structure their work in an effort to maximise their control over the clients, independently of any policy objectives (Lipsky 2010: 58). They also control clients by ensuring that they recognise that their situation is fundamentally different from that of the welfare worker. For instance, clients have to wait at the information desk or in waiting rooms; students have to wear school uniforms and sit in fixed rows of tables; and clients, patients and students can be asked predetermined questions and may be isolated in an effort to prevent them from noticing any structural similarities (or dissimilarities) with other clients, patients or students (Lipsky 2010: 118, 121). Staff thus exercise power when they either let clients wait or handle their case immediately, give or withhold information, asks questions about unnecessary or sensitive aspects of the client's life (Lipsky 2010: 89–93), or, for instance, send clients through the system to either punish or help them or, alternatively, to get rid of job assignments (Lipsky 2010: 132).

Even though Lipsky provides a few examples of how clients can control the work of the staff in bureaucratic organisations, for instance, by taking up too much of the staff's time (Lipsky 2010: 58), he perceives the encounter between the welfare worker and citizens to be one of unidirectional power. This encounter is a Weberian hierarchical structure of authority, in which the capacity of decision-making exclusively belongs to one party (Lipsky 2010: 59) – typically the staff of the bureaucratic organisation. It is thereby especially the rules, procedures and agency of staff (i.e., the ability of staff – not clients – to enforce the rules and procedures) which are the focal points of Lipsky's work. The agency of citizens is secondary, as are the ways in which the two parties are affected by norms outside the bureaucracy, such as how to solve the problems of citizens in ways that will benefit the situation of the citizen, how to define the social problems of citizens and how to secure the voice and choice of citizens. These norms may bear no resemblance to the principles of the bureaucracy but may nevertheless be central for the analysis of encounters in bureaucratic organisations.

Concluding remarks on Lipsky's approach

In bureaucratic organisations, as analysed by Lipsky, staff are constantly considering the ambiguities and contradictions of their performance objectives and consequently form their own ideals of how to solve their clients' problems and deliver the best (possible) service (Lipsky 2010: 144). The principles and rules of the bureaucratic organisation play an important role, as they provide a framework by which the welfare worker can interpret the problems they are supposed to help solve and which may furthermore aid him or her in prioritising among competing (ambiguous) goals (Lipsky 2010: 147). The strong focus on routines, as well as the adherence to procedure, in bureaucratic organisations may cause staff to forget that their actual focus should be on how to obtain the objectives of their work and not (only) to secure that the routines are followed. The emphasis on rules and routines in bureaucratic organisations also means that any attempts to break with these rules or routines may be seen as an effort to attack the entire structure of the organisation (Lipsky 2010: 140), which is why staff in this type of organisation will do their utmost to ensure that routines and rules are followed. When they perform routinised client encounters, they then risk neglecting the agency of (some) citizens. Thus, to follow routines and adhere to rules are their ways of implementing policies and hence acting as political agents, which will automatically cause them to favour the problems of some clients over others, problems that can be solved by this routinised approached (Lipsky 2010: 84). The primary task of the staff is, in other words, to approach and categorise citizens in accordance with the available resources, legislations and principles of the (bureaucratic) organisation in which they work.

However, the routinised and rule-bound encounters in bureaucratic organisations may also be attributed to the expectations of citizens of being greeted and treated as – indeed – clients. This assumption has led to a critique that highlights the (lack of) agency of clients within Lipsky's approach. His theory has also been criticised for being unable to properly address the so-called post-managerial welfare systems (as investigated in the coming analyses on how market values and principles influence the welfare encounter) because of the theory's origins in bureau-professional regimes (Clarke et al. 1994). Lipsky's theory has furthermore been criticised for not properly identifying how discretionary practices can actually be perceived as a series of gradations of freedom for staff to make decisions (Evans and Harris 2004); for not showing how discretion relates to particular 'standards of rationality, fairness and effectiveness' (Dworkin 1978: 33); for not properly distinguishing between different forms of discretions, for instance, administrative discretion, norm discretion, rule discretion and task discretion (Ellis 2011: 223); for not dealing with strong professions, such as doctors, and only dealing with semi-professional groups, such as teachers and social workers (Ellis 2011: 227); for not paying sufficient attention to how discretion is affected by the professional status of the staff involved (Evans 2011: 337–338); and lastly, for not properly relating the study of discretion to a theory of power (Brandon 2005) or – in Huising's (2015) words – the enforcement of authority of professionals on their clients. Despite this broad critique, to this day Lipsky's book still greatly influences many studies conducted in – at first glance – formal, rule-abiding, bureaucratic organisations because of its engagement with practices and its emphasis on how practices in bureaucracies are often interwoven with rules and procedures, as well as discretionary evaluations. As Evans and Harris (2004: 872) state, 'Ideas that are both novel and shed some light on an aspect of the "real world" are something of a rarity. Lipsky's ideas about "street-level bureaucracies" (1980) fall into this category'. The novelty of Lipsky's work is – for the sake of the present argument – his focus on the consequences of ambiguous and conflicting goals for the encounter with the citizen, as well as the dual roles of staff in this encounter.

However, these aforementioned points of critique are obviously relevant if one seeks to conduct a Lipsky-inspired analysis of a bureaucratic organisation and even more so if the organisation in question differs fundamentally from those studied by Lipsky. These points of criticism also serve a different purpose, namely, to strengthen the argument of the need to supplement the work of Lipsky on the bureaucracy with the work of other scholars who study the influence of market values and norms from psychology on the welfare encounter. However, before approaching this literature, other pieces of the literature on the bureaucracy require further attention.

State agents, citizen agents and the agents' two bodies

In order to better understand the discretionary practices that define the work of staff in welfare encounters, Maynard-Moody and Musheno (2000, 2003) investigate a number of stories told by staff in bureaucratic organisations. In their work, they find that welfare workers act as both state agents (who base their judgements on the rules and routines of the bureaucratic organisation) and – more importantly – so-called citizen agents, who base their discretion on their perceptions of the client's individual situation. This distinction between state agent and citizen agent is obviously an analytical one, as staff in practice respond to both the needs of the organisation (the bureaucratic principles and rules) and the situation of the individual citizen (Maynard-Moody and Musheno 2003: 9). As the authors explain, 'This does not mean that rule and policy do not permeate all aspects of street-level work (they do) or that most street-level actions do not conform to agency guidelines (they do as well). ... [However], rules and policy may commonly fit the workers' assessments of citizens and what they need or deserve' (Maynard-Moody and Musheno 2003: 18).

In their study, they find that the discretion of staff was based on their attentiveness to the individual situation of the citizen. This attentiveness was – according to the staff – often the best way for them to make their work both achievable and satisfying. Therefore, instead of defining the welfare encounter as based solely on bureaucratic principles, such as procedures, routines and laws (and hence supporting democratic governance), Maynard-Moody and Musheno (2000) suggest to analyse the encounter as stemming from the interpretations of the individual citizen's situation (as well), because this aspect was one of the most dominant perspectives in their research. In their study, the welfare workers saw themselves first and foremost as a kind of agent for the citizens (and not the state) (Maynard-Moody and Musheno 2000, 2003), a position that also finds support in a recent study of nurses', pedagogues' and teachers' prevention work with families (Harrits and Møller 2014).

When welfare workers act as citizen agents, they are less concerned with if and how their work contributes to policymaking or even if they implement policy. Rather, they explain how their work relates to their conceptualisation of the citizen as either worthy or unworthy of the help offered to them. The study of Maynard-Moody and Musheno thus seems to indicate that welfare work in bureaucratic contexts is a much more normatively grounded practice than what many scholars of so-called street-level bureaucracies have found. Even though responding normatively to the situation of the particular client may render the work life of the welfare worker more difficult and unpleasant, the staff in their study nevertheless emphasised how responding to the needs of the (worthy) citizen was the most rewarding and correct way to respond to a client's needs and problems. Most often, these employees began their career by acting as dutiful state agents but learned, in time, that their decisions about what ought to happen to the citizen were in conflict with the bureaucratic routines of the organisation. For instance, when routines, rules and procedures of the state had to do with closing a case, then the staff wanted to ensure the proper development of their client's case, which they believed they knew due to their relationship with the client (Maynard-Moody and Musheno 2003: 18–21).

This dual role of welfare workers gives them a powerful position: as state agents, they obtain power through their formal positions as doctors, social workers, teachers and so forth, and as citizen agents, they have the power to define what is best for the citizen. The latter role is particularly important in regards to welfare workers, as it points to the necessity of investigating the social order of these encounters, that is, how and which norms, rationales or capitals evoke particular interpretations and 'obvious' ways of categorising the problems of clients. When welfare workers categorise clients as deserving in rehabilitation work and as underserving in police work, or as worthy or unworthy in a number of different settings (Maynard-Moody and Musheno 2003: 23), then these categories point to the social order of the encounter, which stimulates a particular way of interacting and interpreting the actions of the other participant. According to the welfare workers themselves, this categorisation of citizens' problems stemmed from a so-called pragmatic evaluation of what was possible for the individual client (Maynard-Moody and Musheno 2003: 23–24), which was measured against the bureaucratic principles of the welfare encounter.

The ambiguous goals of welfare work were reflected in the multilayered stories told by the welfare workers: 'Street level decision making is complexly moral and contingent rather than narrowly rule bound and fixed. A fundamental dilemma – perhaps the defining characteristics – of welfare work is that the needs of individual citizens-clients exist in tension with the demands and limitations of rules', as Maynard-Moody and Musheno (2003: 93) explain. Therefore, fairness is not only related to bureaucratic principles of treating everyone alike (impartiality) or implementing laws in a procedurally evaluated and correct manner. Rather, fairness entails responding 'to citizen-clients based on their perceived worth', which can be done by giving extraordinary treatment if the client is perceived as a worthy person or, conversely, by abiding by the rules and delaying procedures if the client is deemed unworthy of help. Unlike the treatment of the worthy citizen-clients, bureaucratic rule abidance becomes a way of punishing unworthy clients (Maynard-Moody and Musheno 2003: 93–94, 133).

A dilemma of welfare work is that it does not always make sense for the individual welfare worker (or citizen for that matter) to follow bureaucratic rules and procedures when trying to solve the social problem of a citizen.

A slightly different way of examining this dilemma is by viewing agents of bureaucracies as having 'two bodies': neither an impersonal bureaucrat nor a standardised client, as Dubois (2010: 3) explains. Both welfare workers and citizens are, in other words, social agents who simultaneously have individual personalities and play the part of the stereotypical bureaucrat or client. However, bureaucrats and clients are not forced to act according to the stereotypical perceptions of a bureaucrat or client. For this reason, successful encounters in organisations dominated by bureaucratic principles and rules depend on the agents' abilities to negotiate the stereotypical conceptions of what it means to be a client and a bureaucrat, respectively, and moreover to apply discretion in this negotiation (Dubois 2010: 4; Harrits and Møller 2014).

Staff in bureaucratic organisations thus produce policy rather than implement (Dubois 2010). Staff produce policy on the ground as they 'do more than simply *respond* to performance incentives; they also *adjust* to them as they manage the imbalance between the demands of their jobs and resource constraints' (Brodkin 2011: 272–273 – emphasis in the original). They act both as agents of the state (enforcing rules) and as individual social agents with their own unique personalities.

However, it is not only bureaucratic principles and rules – and the way in which staff translate these rules and principles – that are key in the analysis of the encounter between welfare workers and citizens in bureaucratic organisations. More and more studies show how citizens also take on an active role in defining the problem at stake and how it should be solved. Citizens hold many roles in today's welfare encounter: they are perceived and view themselves as 'customers, co-producers, clients etc. and all of these identities (including the identity as client) imply forms of agency – ways of acting – that are [even] prescribed, or at least presumed, in formal policy statements' (Prior and Barnes 2011: 267). In other words, citizens do not merely take on bureaucratic identities and interpret their situation in administrative terms, such as to live with a cohabitant, to have the wrong code or to experience the absence of sustained affective ties, as shown in Dubois' (2010: 23–24) work. They do interpret their situation in accordance with bureaucratic principles and categories, but they also enter the welfare situation with expectations of what this encounter should be all about, expectations which are not affected only by bureaucratic principles and which affect the other party of the encounter as well.

Even though some scholarly work – that of Dubois (2010), for instance – focuses more on the agency of citizens than do many Lipsky-inspired studies, their agency is nevertheless primarily reflecting the rules of the bureaucratic setting (first-order agency). These studies deal with a type of agency that illustrates how citizens respond to the bureaucratic framework, a type of agency that, of course, is important to examine but nevertheless is largely overlooked within Lipsky-inspired studies. However, neither in the work of Dubois nor in the broad literature presently cited does one find analyses of how the behaviour of citizens may affect the staff and hence the bureaucratic encounter by bringing norms and expectations developed outside the bureaucracy into the encounter.

Concluding comments: the role of agency in a bureaucratic context

Most of the classic work on how bureaucracies function – as seen from the front line – reveals how the principles and rules of bureaucracies affect the work of the staff, their ambiguous roles towards the citizens and (primarily) the categorisation of the social problems of citizens within this type of organisation (Maynard-Moody and Musheno 2003; Lipsky 2010; Ellis 2011). Most studies focus on the dilemmas of bureaucrats, which stem from their efforts to provide individually oriented help or service (McBeath and Webb 2002; Lymbery 2003; Evans and Harris 2004). These dilemmas have in Lipsky-inspired studies been approached as stemming from the rule-abiding and formal structures of bureaucracies with ties to a Weberian perception of the ideal-type bureaucracy in which the trained official (welfare worker) holds a superior position (Weber 2013: 991–992). These studies have developed nuanced perceptions of how one may perceive the encounter between staff and citizens by assuming that the principles and rules of bureaucratic organisation strongly influence the practices within these organisations. In such cases, it is the administrative aspects of the staff's work (e.g., to secure impartiality by routinizing practices) which automatically become central to the analysis (e.g., Brehm and Gates 1997), challenged and supplemented, of course, by analyses of the soft power of the many discretionary decisions, which all confront the assumed goal of, for instance, impartiality. In any case, the principles of the bureaucratic organisation – mediated through its staff – are key in Lipsky-inspired analyses, as they are assumed to produce bureaucratic norm-infused practices, which then are either supported or resisted by the encountering welfare workers and citizens.

Within this branch of Lipsky-inspired research, there are also several studies which explicitly seek to relate discretionary practices with a concept of power and which centre around the role of welfare workers. Key questions in relation to these studies are, for instance, whether welfare workers are to be perceived as powerful practitioners who undermine the established policies with their discretion-based decisions (Baldwin 2000), whether the discretionary practices of welfare workers are better perceived as necessary reactions to a structurally anchored paradoxical reality that 'produce[s] possible contradictory action imperatives' (Hupe and Hill 2007: 296), whether discretionary practices are to be perceived as the only way in which welfare workers may ensure high professional standards in their work (Lewis and Glennerster 1996) or, finally, whether discretion is to be perceived as a tool to be used against the interest of the citizens (Horwath 2000).

As these questions suggest, there seems to be a general scholarly interest in examining how and why welfare workers exercise discretion (Evans and Harris 2004: 891). This focus on agency is qualified in a later publication by Maynard-Moody and Musheno (2012), who urge scholars to move beyond the so-called state agent or implementation–control–discretion narrative (Maynard-Moody and Musheno 2012: 18). They argue that the action component of discretionary practices is central to such analyses, as discretion involves agency: 'to form judgements and take actions is inherent. It is not delegated or legitimated by laws, rules or procedures, but is an essential aspect of being human ... [because no acts] exist apart from social systems' (Maynard-Moody and Musheno 2012: 19). In order to examine the soft power of the normative demands of welfare workers' jobs and in an effort to avoid treating welfare workers as merely policy implementers, they suggest viewing the practices in bureaucratic organisations as rooted in pragmatic improvisation rather than discretionary decision-making (Maynard-Moody and Musheno 2012: 18). They believe that the concept of pragmatic improvisation will emphasise agency and thus create a different framework for examining the many situations in which there is a mismatch between the rules of an organisation and the problems of its clients. Quoting Brodkin, Maynard-Moody and Musheno state that welfare workers 'don't do what they want, they do what they can' (Brodkin 2011: 27 in Maynard-Moody and Musheno 2012: 12). According to them, what welfare workers '"can do" is to improvise and these pragmatic improvisations are thus an expression of their agency within the context of the rules, practices and roles' (Maynard-Moody and Musheno 2012: 20).

In order to gain a better understanding of both the influence of citizens on the welfare encounter and how norms outside the bureaucracy affect this meeting, it may be necessary to develop a research design more sensitive to the voices of citizens and that can better capture how norms outside the bureaucracy affect the encounter. There is a need for a research design that regards both welfare workers and citizens as reflexive subjects to a greater degree than seems to be the case today (Prior and Barnes 2011: 267). Chapter 6 will centre around how the values of the market and NPM affect the encounter in (bureaucratic) settings such as welfare work.

Note

1. In order to harmonise the concepts used in this book (and thus ease the reading), I have decided to primarily use the terms of *staff* and *welfare worker* instead of *street-level bureaucrat* or *street-level worker*, which in this Lipsky-tradition are the most commonly used concepts. I have also decided to use the terms *clients* and *citizens* interchangeably.

6

The market context: service–consumer

Introduction

> Consumer/customer do not fit as I do not 'buy'. Service user is politically correct psychobabble. Citizen is not a word that appeals to me. When I need treatment I am a patient, when I do not I am a member of the public. (Patient cited in Clarke *et al.* 2007: 130)

Even though scholars may not use the term *psychobabble*, as this patient does, when reflecting on the concept of the service user in health settings, scholars have nevertheless – and for a long time – criticised the ideal of service in citizens' encounters with welfare workers. In his famous book *Asylums* first published in 1961 (1974) based on fieldwork in a US state hospital, Goffman presents a thorough critique of a service ideal in work with psychiatric patients, a theme he readdressed some 20 years later in his presidential address to the American Sociological Association in 1982. Here he problematised how the interactional order of service implies the rule of equal and courteous treatment, which cannot always be practised in service transactions and even less so in the encounters between clients/patients and welfare workers (Goffman 1983: 14–15). Today, the issue still carries great importance; especially when recognising that different concepts and norms bring different identifications of the individual and the relationship into play. This chapter consequently focuses on market values and takes a closer look at how service and other ideals affect the encounter between citizens and welfare workers.

The chapter begins by introducing the market context and its inherent principles, followed by a discussion of how the marketisation of public administration lays the groundwork for a number of challenges and dilemmas for both welfare workers and citizens (Mayo 2013). It covers the ways in which the standards, benchmarks, guidelines, incentive structures and other aspects of NPM, combined with business values such as competition, choice and flexibility, have affected the encounter between the welfare worker and the citizen (Kuhlmann *et al.* 2009). Finally, the chapter discusses the role of the soft power of equality and courtesy in these idealised service encounters and concludes with a discussion on agency in market-inspired welfare work.

The market context and different areas of welfare work

The current and strengthened focus on service in the welfare encounter has led scholars to suggest that Western countries have changed from being welfare societies to active societies in which citizens may only gain access to social rights if they are willing to take charge of their own lives and be responsible, active citizens (OECD 1997; Dwyer 2004: 268). In addition and with regard to the staff of welfare organisations, this literature suggests a new way of describing the roles of welfare workers, as they no longer have to deal first and foremost with bureaucratic principles and compensate for the ambiguities in their work by engaging in discretionary practices (as shown in Chapter 5). Today, welfare workers are instead expected to act as business and service entrepreneurs with a 'can do' attitude (McCafferty 2010), sales personnel and other social roles associated with the market context. Some scholars argue that this development aims at creating so-called entrepreneurial spirit in particular areas of public administration and seeks to establish an overall enterprising agenda in today's active societies in an effort to 'ultimately [create] a society of global entrepreneurial citizens' (McCafferty 2010: 546). Consequently, the citizen is perceived and approached as an agent who knows what he or she wants and is capable of making choices – as opposed to the (democratic) citizen of the past, who merely supported the pursuit of public interests (DeLeon and Denhardt 2000: 91). A popular and illustrative slogan of the market context is 'steer don't row' (DeLeon and Denhardt 2000: 90), in other words, to set a direction for the individual person, who then does whatever needs to be done in an effort to reach the desired goal, be it employment, substance independence or other preferred ways of being and behaving.

As discussed, welfare work covers a wide range of activities: social workers encounter problematic families, police officers encounter (potential) criminals, teachers encounter students and so on. For this reason, the ways in which the different areas of welfare work are influenced by market principles and values will necessarily differ tremendously. The research of Clarke and colleagues (2007: 63–64) shows, for instance, that within the area of health there is a strong focus on the individual, whereas within policing there is a strong focus on community. Thus, the ideal typical citizen varies from the individual choice-making patient, user or consumer within health and social care to the collective being the agent within policing. Just as the particular welfare area is of great importance (e.g., health or policing), it is also important to consider whether the participants are able to voice their situations and opinions (as is expected of the market context's ideal-type customers) or if they in fact are vulnerable citizens, such as poor people, the elderly and the disabled, who are less inclined or even unable to do so.

Thus, to integrate a market rationale in welfare work has real effects. However, this chapter refrains from explicating how these effects relate to particular welfare areas and citizen groups. To do so is without a doubt a both important and interesting endeavour, but it nevertheless falls outside the aim of giving a broader introduction to the consequences of integrating market principles in welfare work.

New Public Management and New Public Service

Ever since NPM was introduced more systematically as a management technology in Western countries in the 1980s, there has been an expansion of researchers examining how market values have affected welfare work and the encounters with citizens (e.g., DeLeon and Denhardt 2000; Fountain 2001; Clarke *et al.* 2007; Jos and Tompkins 2009). A recurring theme in these studies is how the market context has increasingly transformed the citizen of the state or the client of the bureaucracy into a consumer or customer of the market and, consequently, how this transformation has led to a wide range of problems for both the citizen (as indicated in the opening quote) and the welfare worker. For instance, this newly arisen emphasis on customer service within welfare work has created a dilemma of how to increase the efficiency and responsiveness of public services without it being detrimental to the democracy (Fountain 2001: 60).

Hence, it is not only the techniques of NPM (e.g., standards and benchmarks), which have been accused of challenging key fundamental principles of the democracy and have been regarded as methods, which may lead to a deskilling of the staff in public organisations (Baines 2004: 24). The service norms of equality and courtesy (Goffman 1983: 14–15) and the business values of the market, such as competition, choice, flexibility and respect for the entrepreneurial spirit, have similarly been criticised for their inability to be integrated in the tenets of welfare work in public organisations (DeLeon and Denhardt 2000: 91; McCafferty 2010). Denhardt and Denhardt (2003: 5) find, for instance, that although some 'techniques have proven helpful, the quick translation of business values into the public sector raises substantial and troubling questions that public officials should consider with great care'. Some scholars even suggest that market principles have come to dominate welfare principles and that the welfare society has changed into an active society (Taylor-Gooby 2004: 33), or what has been termed a Third Way within the UK (Dwyer 2004: 268).

A Third Way approach to the citizen conceptualises a new political approach to welfare work that relies on neither an unfettered market nor the classic bureaucratic top-down control. Former Prime Minister Tony Blair argued, for instance, that service providers in the UK should take on this new approach to the citizen that combines principles and values from business, neoliberalism and socialism (Clarke *et al.* 2007). The Third Way approach has moreover inspired a number of other welfare states to introduce policies, which aim at securing and solidifying this new perspective on the citizen. However, the approach has also been criticised for being a cover-up for pulling back the welfare state and hence reducing its costs.

Whether or not scholars perceive this Third Way approach as strongly reflecting market principles, most of them would agree that it is an approach which reflects a stronger integration of market thinking in welfare work than previously. For example, the activation of the citizen (and the imposed responsibility) has in some research been related to the expansion of private providers in public administration, for instance, the privatisation of the UK job centres. However, the privatisation of unemployment programmes has led to critique that points to the fact that this new way of dealing with unemployment actually neglects the demand side, and thus works from the assumption that jobs are available if only the unemployed citizen becomes more active in his or her efforts to obtain a job (Grover 2009). This critique emphasises the tendency to focus on the individual (and his or her resources and capabilities) rather than the collective (e.g., the structure of the labour market and how it may prevent certain groups of unemployed citizens from gaining employment). It captures the preference of the market to interpret (the actions of) individuals by viewing their interests (or lack thereof) in solving their problematic unemployment situations. The privatisation of employment schemes – or, for instance, of care for the elderly or disabled – is thus interrelated with the introduction of a Third Way approach and its idea of citizens as active. It is an approach that regards social problems as predominantly individualised problems and consequently turns to the individual citizens in search for how to solve these (individualised) problems.

The individualisation of social problems has also been conceptualised as the personalisation approach: a method that in a similar way positions the citizen as active and explicitly takes a non-paternalistic and non-hierarchical approach to the citizen in an effort to make citizens (or service users, as they are also often called) responsible for their own situations. However, according to some scholars, the personalisation approach 'amounts to nothing more than a covert strategy for importing market techniques into public services' (Mladenov *et al.* 2015: 309), such as the improved match between users and services, cost-effectiveness and efficiency (Spicker 2013). This and other points of criticism of the personalisation approach to the citizen will be dealt with in greater detail in Chapter 7 on the psychology-inspired context of welfare work.

It is not only the expansion of private service providers within public administration that is linked to the dominance of market principles in welfare work. The many reforms of schools, hospitals and social benefits programmes – conceptualised as NPM and thus inspired by the private sector's focus on standards against which to measure output, ensure a high quality of work and evaluate the amount of money spent in (or on) the public sector – are also examples of how a market mindset has found its way into welfare work (Hood 1991). Such reforms, alongside the perception of citizens as customers or consumers who are assumed to be in pursuit of their own particular interests, may render the encounter with the citizen quite challenging. This has to do with the fact that citizens' responses and reactions to the various welfare reforms may not come across as policy-rational, which is the dominant type of rationality among staff working in public administration. In other words, (welfare) customer services assume a particular type of agent, that is, someone who thinks and argues in line with how the welfare worker thinks and argues. However, assumptions of citizens (and welfare work) as economic-rational, legal-rational or policy-rational may be a gross oversimplification of both the context in which the welfare work takes place and the possible interpretations of people's actions (Fountain 2001: 66).

Some scholars have suggested the concept of New Public Service (NPS) to emphasise that public servants are ideally 'building relationships of trust and collaborations with and among citizens ... [rather than] respond[ing] to the selfish, short-term interest of "customers"' as assumed in NPM (Denhardt and Denhardt 2000: 555). These NPS scholars suggest that welfare workers should focus on more than the market and the techniques and principles of NPM (Denhardt and Denhardt 2000: 555). They furthermore point to a number of issues, which the market context cannot explain, for instance, that individuals also view themselves as democratic citizens with public interests, which greatly contradicts the belief of NPM (in which a person is chiefly motivated by his or her self-interests) (Denhardt and Denhardt 2000: 557). Thus, within the frame of NPM both producers and consumers of welfare services are seen as driven by self-interest (Clarke *et al.* 2007: 30). The NPS regard NPM values such as efficiency, productivity and control with much criticism: 'Values such as efficiency and productivity should not be lost, but should be placed in the larger context of democracy, community and the public interest', as Denhardt and Denhardt (2000: 557) argue.

Although there are differences between NPM and NPS, they may be perceived as one perspective due to their joint focus on the effects and benefits of a market rationale within public administration or welfare work. After all, the two approaches show more similarities than differences. The following section takes a closer look at some of the ideas behind these NPM/NPS-inspired reforms, which most Western countries have been subjected to since the 1980s onwards and which have been discussed by using concepts such as marketisation, privatisation, contractualisation, managerialisation, decentralisation and collaboration (Clarke *et al.* 2007: 42). The aim is to shed light on the positions or roles available to both citizens and welfare workers in encounters regulated by NPM/NPS and other market principles and values.

Citizen-consumers, entrepreneurial selves and active citizens

As the title of Clarke and colleagues' (2007) book *Creating Citizen-Consumers* refers to, the welfare recipients of today are approached and understood as both citizens and consumers. This hyphenated identity consists of two identities that are usually not combined. To be a citizen is a political construct in which, for instance, equality before the law is paramount. To be a consumer is, however, an economic construct in which the individual is understood from a market rationale as someone who is engaged in economic transactions and is capable of selectively choosing among different programmes, services and so forth (Clarke *et al.* 2007: 2). The citizen-consumer is, in other words, an identity that bridges the public sphere and its practices (related to, e.g., state, public, political, collective, de-commodification and rights) with the private sphere and its practices (associated with, e.g., market, private, economical, individual, commodification and exchange) (Clarke *et al.* 2007: 3).

The reference to consumers and customers – and, not to forget, their interacting partners, namely, service providers, sellers and entrepreneurs (welfare workers) – when examining the welfare encounter may obviously lay the ground for problems. For instance, the choices of the (welfare) consumer are restricted by a variety of things (such as imperfect information and lack of customer mobility), just as the welfare workers face many constraints in their role as a salesperson within welfare work in regards to adverse selection, price fixing and so on (Jos and Tompkins 2009: 1077). This ideal typical model of sellers and consumers within welfare work distorts the very matter being discussed because this role pair shows so little resemblance to the actual encounter between citizens and welfare workers. It moreover brings about practices which may have negative effects on the welfare work, such as self-policing and the privatisation of client complaints (Baines 2004: 15). Sellers in traditional service companies are in a position that allows them to both cream and discard their customers, a work description that is hardly an ideal point of departure for welfare work (Jos and Tompkins 2009: 1078), even though creaming does occur, as discussed by Lipsky (2010: 107–108).

By reviewing the literature on the relationship or transactions between customers and sellers in the public sphere, as well as the literature on private transactions, Jos and Tompkins (2009: 1077–1078) conclude that although there may be many similarities between the transactions within the public sector and the private sector, these two types of transactions are, nevertheless, 'significantly, perhaps fundamentally, different'. The authors turn their attention to the public service principles at play in encounters between professionals and clients, guardians and wards, facilitators and citizens or consumers and salespersons and discuss the normative principles embedded in these various role pairs and how they may lead to dilemmas in welfare work (Jos and Tompkins 2009: 1081–1083). To ensure public service norms in these very different fields and relationships means 'stepping outside the managerial zone of control into territory where the relationship between what providers do and what citizens want is unknown and trying to create value there' (Jos and Tompkins 2009: 1083).

Thus, to be identified (and to identify oneself) as a client, patient, citizen or consumer – or likewise as a professional, facilitator, service provider or salesperson – brings about complex identity work, as each identification automatically leads to different expectations, such as passive (client), in need of help (patient), equal (citizen) or capable of making choices (consumer). The same person may 'combine being a knowledgeable expert of their own condition; a rights-bearing and assertive citizen; an anxious dependent and a seeker after professional help and advice' (Clarke *et al.* 2007: 67). These roles and footings are identifications that give meaning to – and derive meaning from – the context in which they are produced, as discussed in Chapter 4 with reference to the scholarly work on institutional identities (e.g., Gubrium and Holstein 2001). The welfare encounter thus involves a high level of complexity, as public servants may serve more than one public constituency or 'serve individuals in multiple capacities', as Jos and Tompkins (2009: 1081) argue.

However, the identification as citizen-consumer may actually empower citizens as they – by viewing themselves as ideal typical consumers – are then liberated from the traditional paternalistic power of the welfare state over clients and patients, which may lead to a more power-balanced encounter with staff in public service organisation. However, this type of reasoning stems from the belief that practices within public services reflect a political rationality (Rose and Miller 2010). In this case that citizens are able to challenge welfare workers and position themselves as responsible individuals, as someone who is able to make the right (policy/market-rational) choices (as evaluated by the welfare worker) (Clarke *et al.* 2007: 24). However, individuals positioned as consumers may not behave as such if the other identifications available to them appear more favourable or appropriate, just as bureaucrats and their clients do not necessarily behave in the manner prescribed by the bureaucracy (Clarke *et al.* 2007: 17; Dubois 2010; Lipsky 2010). With reference to the opening quote of this chapter, it seems fair to assume that the idea of the liberating consumer identification does not apply to all clients or patients in welfare work, who may find the idea of service users an example of 'politically correct psychobabble'.

Another key aspect of the marketisation of welfare work is the notion of the entrepreneurial self, which is a metaphor that describes the influence of market principles in a slightly different way (Rose 1999; DeLeon and Denhardt 2000; Bröckling 2015). The entrepreneurial self sheds light on the effect of mutating citizens into consumers through the 'politics of the contract' (Clarke *et al.* 2007), similar to the contracts between buyers and sellers. The idea of entrepreneurial selves thus points to the strengthened focus in present-day welfare work to make citizens responsible for their own situations in synchronicity with the (sometimes hidden) agenda of retracting the welfare state (Richardson *et al.* 2014: 1716). An example hereof is the so-called community contracts, which are often 'quasi-legal arrangements that involve both citizens and welfare workers in tackling social problems through agreed responsibilities (Richardson *et al.* 2014: 1716). These community contracts strengthen the portion of the citizen that has to do with service, as they clarify both the standard of services that he or she can expect to receive and whether the existing service standards are met (Andersen 2007; Richardson *et al.* 2014: 1726). These contracts have potentially empowering effects for the service providers, as well as the citizens or residents of a community. The entrepreneurial self is a citizen identification that emphasises the rights and responsibilities of present-day citizens. This identity is thus a very diffident identity than the bureaucracy's (passive) client. This shift from bureaucratic to liberal rule also changes the traditional power relations of expertise by assigning the expert position to the citizen (Rose 1999: 164–165 in Clarke *et al.* 2007: 20). The welfare worker is thereby no longer the sole expert in the relationship with the client or patient, as both the welfare worker and the citizen may identify with an entrepreneurial role and thus think of new ways of how to deal with the problem or situation at hand.

Another way of talking about citizens in welfare work saturated by market principles is by referring to citizens as active. For instance, do people see themselves as job seekers or as unemployed? Do they actively take responsibility for their situation or do they passively wait for the welfare workers to solve their problems (Clarke *et al.* 2007: 20–22)? To perceive the welfare recipient as an active citizen also affects the ways in which the welfare workers think about and relate to their work: are they actually able to work with citizens positioned as active, that is, people who take initiative to resolve their issues? Are welfare workers capable of taking upon themselves the role of the mediator, facilitator and coach (Denhardt and Denhardt 2003: 8) and not merely the expert? As these questions indicate, the marketisation of welfare work produces new expectations of citizens, as well as welfare workers, who thereby become in need of new skills, such as 'brokering, negotiating and conflict resolution', when dealing with the active citizen (Denhardt and Denhardt 2003: 9). The marketisation of welfare work hereby creates a strong expectation of rearranging public services in a manner so that they become (even more) user led and not led primarily by the welfare workers or the rules of the bureaucracy. This shift towards market mechanisms can be seen as a way of positioning the citizen as a sovereign consumer that produces a different dynamic within public services driven by the user, the patient or the client and not the government or the welfare worker (Clarke *et al.* 2007: 44–45).

However, Lucio (2009) points to a slightly different way of analysing the marketisation of welfare work and the current reframing of citizenship. He focuses on the passifying effect the role of recipients of services may have. Lucio argues that the service encounter 'limits the role of citizens to mere recipients of services rather than active participants' (Lucio 2009: 880). In analysing the idea of customers within welfare work and the customer approach to the citizen, he identifies some of the same problems as mentioned by other authors, for instance, that certain groups of vulnerable citizens (poor people, immigrants, etc.) are excluded from the customer model of citizenship. For instance, and as shown in a study on the access of disadvantaged citizens to legal services (Mayo 2013), not all citizens were able to pay for the service they needed and not all citizens were able to take upon themselves the role of the expert (i.e., someone who knows what is best for himself or herself).

Expert citizens

As indicated, market-inspired thinking within welfare work may produce inequality, as the most demanding consumers – those who are able to voice their situation – will receive the most attention from the welfare worker. The encounter between citizens and welfare workers is therefore influenced (and challenged) by (at least) two important factors: firstly, that the citizens who push to be heard and understood by the (busy) welfare worker may come first in line for service (help), and secondly, that the idea of expert citizens confronts a norm of expertise that has traditionally placed the welfare worker in the role of the professional (expert) and thus in the role of knowing what is best. Because the welfare workers have historically been positioned as the more *knowledgeable* party, one must assume that the personal experiences of the citizen are not regarded as equal or even comparable to the professional expertise of welfare workers (Clarke *et al.* 2007: 100) – this despite the recent talk about (and wish for) the so-called expert citizens. 'Users may know what they think they want, only professional expertise can establish what is necessary', as Clarke and colleagues (2007: 112) state. Thus, if the citizen is able to talk about his or her situation in a way that will be perceived by the welfare worker as expert knowledge in its own right (even though it is based on personal experiences), then this will place the citizen in a powerful position. However, a number of studies have found that this is not usually the case, the main problem being that what a citizen believes himself or herself to need may not correspond with the assessments of the welfare worker or even be possible for the welfare worker to provide (Clarke *et al.* 2007: 114). There are difficult balancing acts at play between lay knowledge and expertise in the welfare encounter, a confrontation between lay, situated and experienced knowledge and the so-called objective (expert) knowledge of professionals (Clarke *et al.* 2007: 115). Clarke and colleagues (2007: 115) consequently state that 'there has been a reluctance to accede to the claim that "professionals know best" – instead people have laid claim to being "experts of their own condition"'.

The expert citizen is ideally a reasonable, responsible and realistic individual (Clarke *et al.* 2007: 116), qualities which illustrate that this identity is difficult (or even downright impossible) to define in any unambiguous, non-normative way. To be realistic and reasonable is to act in a way that shows that you not only understand and accept the organisational and occupational (policy) rationale of the welfare worker whom you encounter, but also applaud their actions and decisions. The notion of citizens as active agents who are capable of making reasonable and responsible choices in their lives thus calls for further attention to the differences between citizens, for instance, how their gender, age, ethnicity and social class affect the encounter, as these factors may limit the agency of citizens. In summary, the market context's new agents – citizen-consumers, entrepreneurs, active citizens and expert citizens – illustrates what DeLeon and Denhardt (2000) call a reinvention movement in today's transformation of public administrations in a number of Western countries.

Reinventing welfare work

With reference to Osborne and Gaebler's book *Reinventing Government* from 1992, DeLeon and Denhardt (2000) suggest the term the *reinvention movement* to shed light on what they perceive as a type of denial of citizenship in ncustomised welfare work today. As already established, the market context rests on the notion that both clients and welfare workers act in accordance with their own self-interests, which is thought to automatically maximise the common social good (DeLeon and Denhardt 2000: 91). However, according to DeLeon and Denhardt, this description is far from how welfare work actually functions in reality, as in markets people actually compete; they do not cooperate. Hence, by introducing the concept of the reinvention movement, they wish to emphasise how the consumer culture – when introduced into welfare work – confronts basic democratic principles such as citizenship, civic engagement and public interest (DeLeon and Denhardt 2000: 96). The rise of a consumer culture has to do with authority, at least if one chooses to focus on the choice of consumers. Consumer culture and the positioning of citizens as consumers – instead of, for instance, bureaucratic clients – thus point to important power issues as the service model challenges the bureaucratic way of organising authority (Clarke *et al.* 2007: 11).

The focus on citizens' ability to consume and choose among the different welfare offers, as well as the notion that citizens and welfare workers are engaged in an equal, power-balanced and courteous relationship, excludes – as mentioned – certain individuals and groups of citizens. The excluded citizens are those who lack financial resources, who cannot consume and who live a very different life from the (middle-class) welfare workers and their particular norms and ideas. According to Clarke and colleagues (2007: 13) and with reference to Baumann, such citizens are excluded in multiple ways: 'from the activities of consumption, from the exercise of choice and from the moral realm of the worthy'. Their actions are no longer evaluated according to a work ethic but are instead evaluated according to a so-called aesthetic of consumption. When citizens are offered the position of consumer or customer of welfare services, their social problems are then individualised and become a matter of choice. In this process, not only is the citizen transformed from a client into a customer but also welfare issues are transformed from being part of the larger public sphere to solely belonging to the private sphere, from being an issue of the state to being an issue of the market (Clarke *et al.* 2007: 17). The hyphenated identity of citizen-consumer can consequently be perceived as produced by a so-called anti-welfareism, which is a perception that holds that market mechanisms will not foster the demoralising dependency culture that the welfare state has created (Clarke *et al.* 2007: 29).

Concluding comments: the role of agency in a market context

There is no doubt that NPM and the marketisation of welfare work have to do with effectivity, lowering cost and so on. However, a market context is also about strengthening the agency of citizens in the encounter with welfare workers. The soft power that regulates the encounter in the market context thus urges citizens to take on the position of someone who is active, can voice his or her situation and make 'relevant' choices. The welfare worker is equally regulated by soft and powerful mechanisms, which grant expertise to citizens who behave as experts. These citizens voice their situation and make choices that – from a social policy perspective – are deemed as relevant. It is, in other words, not all types of (active) citizen behaviour that are welcome in the welfare encounter, and not all citizens are – from a resource perspective – able to take on this demanding role. The marketisation context thus leaves no room for the vulnerable or 'irrational' client or patient, who either is incapable of voicing his or her situation or fails to adhere to the dominant market rationale. Furthermore, the market context leaves no room for citizens who are unable to formulate a solution to their problems. The soft power at work is the capitals and rationales of the market that define which behaviours of both welfare workers and citizens are appropriate. Consequently, the assumption of a particular type of market-rational agent may not capture the implications of welfare work very well (and be applicable to all citizens or welfare workers), which is why many scholars argue that the emphasis of a market rationale in welfare work cannot predominantly be regarded as a positive thing (Taylor-Gooby 1999; DeLeon and Denhardt 2000; Clarke *et al.* 2007; Jos and Tompkins 2009).

This critique of what it takes to be perceived as a rational individual relates, of course, not only to welfare work. It is a universal feature of human interaction that individuals adjust their actions so that they can be understood and perceived as (contextually) rational by the people with whom they interact. Or put differently, as human beings, individuals are continuously trying to define what the encounters – in which they engage or should engage in – are all about (the possibility for second-order agency). When a definition other than their own defines or frames the encounter, and when this definition is elevated to an expression of rational action, then the participating individuals either try to change the definition or adjust their behaviour according to the winning definition, as discussed in Chapter 4 with reference to the work of Goffman and other symbolic interactionists.

The critical question is therefore, who gets to define what to expect from encounters between citizens and welfare workers? Or in other words, whose expectations of both welfare workers and citizens will produce the most substantial consequences for the interacting parties? There is no doubt that the market context is currently quite powerful, as it produces a political agenda that positions citizens as agents who ought to make choices, take responsibility and voice their situation; it thus defines rational behaviour according to these norms. The reason why this agenda has been accepted (at least to some extent) into welfare work has to do with two possible factors: firstly, if citizens are active in solving their problems and act in accordance with the expectations of the welfare workers, then this will automatically become the quick (and cost-effective) way of solving the problems of citizens. Secondly, the emphasis on citizens to take responsibility and be proactive is likely rooted in a desire to be rid of the much criticised patronising welfare state (and staff) of the past, as well as the (historically anchored) practice of distinguishing between 'deserving' and 'undeserving' poor, or between those who suffer from bad luck and those who are in need because they fail to take responsibility for themselves (Ryan 2007). However, and as many of the cited studies illustrate, this (new) positioning of citizens as responsible may not be applicable for all citizens, because it is without a doubt quite a demanding position to take on. Additionally, it can be equally demanding for the welfare workers, who then have to abandon their position as experts and engage with the citizen in a more coaching and facilitating manner. Chapter 7 therefore centres around the ways in which a psychological context, that emphasises welfare workers' coaching and facilitation of citizens, frames the welfare encounter.

7

The psychology-inspired context:
coach–coachee

Introduction

The doctor [is] not just a physician but adviser, the nurse [is] not just [a] carer
but trainer, patients [are] more than consumers – [they are] partners. (Former
Prime Minister Gordon Brown cited in Needham 2011: 141)

Today's welfare work is not only influenced by principles of the bureaucracy
(Chapter 5) or the market (Chapter 6), as the quote from former Prime
Minister Gordon Brown illustrates; both welfare workers and citizens
are expected to take on the roles of advisers, trainers and partners as
well. Current welfare work can as such be seen as equally influenced by
norms from psychology. This has led to an increased research interest in
how psychology and more therapeutic person-centred approaches affect
the welfare work. The title of this chapter – 'The psychology-inspired
context' – seeks to cover a range of both different and partly overlapping discussions regarding various ways of identifying the welfare state,
such as therapeutic (Polsky 1991; Chriss 1999), psychological (Jones
et al. 2013), maternal (Pykett 2012), or pedagogised (Pykett 2010;
Singh 2015), alongside discussions of the so-called personalisation and
co-production approaches to welfare work (e.g., Bovaird 2007; Needham
and Glasby 2015).

The focus on norms from psychology does not imply that one should turn
one's back on the classic issues of the welfare state altogether. However, a
research focus on the therapeutic, pedagogical and more person-centred
approaches to the citizen will allow for analyses that supplement those of
the bureaucratic or market-oriented approaches. Thus, when applying a
psychological perspective to the welfare encounter, particular themes and
ways of perceiving the citizen come to the forefront. From this perspective,
we are no longer dealing with the client of the bureaucracy or the consumer
of the market, and welfare workers are neither bureaucratic administrators

nor service providers. Instead, scholars emphasise the prevalence of norms from psychology in an effort to show how the roles of welfare workers, such as facilitators, coaches and therapists, are at play even in welfare areas such as employment, which traditionally are not associated with the so-called 'psy' disciplines (such as psychology, psychiatry and medicine) (Rose 1998).

Similar to the market approach, an individualised psychology-inspired approach regards the citizen as someone who is able to voice his or her problems and knows (or will learn to know) how to solve them in a manner consistent with the evaluations and judgements of the welfare worker. Similarly, this approach perceives the welfare worker as someone who strives to become the best possible personal adviser, coach, counsellor and support for his or her clients (Leadbetter and Lownsbrough 2005: 38). We are, in other words, dealing with Habermas' (1984) description of an ideal speech situation, which entails a position of equal power between the communicating parties, a position free from both physical and psychological coercion. However, much research has shown that this description bears very little resemblance to real-life (welfare) interactions: welfare workers are expected to be able to manage the ambiguous position of being both an empathic coach or facilitator (who refrains from judging the life of the citizen) and a professional (who assumes a traditional expert role and helps the citizen resolve his or her problem). In some ways, this role ambiguity very much resembles the ambiguous roles of administrators or bureaucrats, as discussed in Chapter 5.

These psychology-inspired roles place the citizens 'at the heart of service, enabling them to become participants in the design and delivery' of the welfare work (Ferguson 2007: 392). However, this approach to welfare work has been criticised in two specific regards, which resemble the critique aimed at the market-inspired context: firstly, for individualising and privatising the (social) problems of unemployed people, homeless people, children with behavioural issues and so on (Järvinen and Mik-Meyer 2003; Leadbetter and Lownsbrough 2005), and secondly, for positioning the citizen as an expert, as doing so challenges the classic expert status of the welfare staff (Ferguson 2007: 399), unless he or she succeeds in making the citizen adopt the agenda and norms of the welfare workers. This chapter addresses these issues and begins by introducing the variety of scholarly work on the therapeutic state, the psychological state, the pedagogical state and so forth. Hereafter, the approaches of personalisation and co-production will be discussed, followed by a discussion of the agency of both welfare workers and citizens and how they each respond to this particular framing of the welfare work.

The therapeutic state

> The therapeutic ethos has become a taken-for-granted part of everyday life. It provides culture with a set of symbols and codes that determine the boundaries of moral life. ... The helping professions ... attempt to instil prosocial adjustments in individuals who, for whatever reason, have taken a wrong turn in life. (Chriss cited in Nolan 1998: 6)

As this quote suggests, the work conducted by welfare staff – the so-called helping professionals – is today guided by a therapeutic ethos. This particular ethos is prevalent not only in clinics, hospitals and other psy settings (Rose 1998), but even steers the welfare work conducted in schools, prisons, job centres and other government institutions (Chriss 1999: 7). With inspiration from symbolic interactionism and the work of Goffman, Chriss (1999: 8) argues that this medicalisation of everyday life may cause an unfortunate disempowerment of citizens whose perceptions of their own problems do not correspond with how the fields of psychology, psychiatry or medicine perceive and respond to such issues.

By using the concept of the therapeutic state, scholars want to emphasise the dominance of a medical model and its particular ideology within current welfare states (Chriss 1999). Such scholars argue, and have done for a long time, that welfare workers' goal with the encounter with the citizen is to try to make him or her adjust to the (psychological) norms of modern society, such as, to engage in healthy relationships and develop a positive sense of self (Polsky 1991: 3). The key underlying assumption in this type of welfare work is that many citizens require intervention because they are incapable of governing their own lives. Thus, the state must 'normalize' them so that they can (re)enter the social mainstream (Polsky 1991: 4).

This focus on how particular norms from psychology affect the welfare encounter is still central in much literature and is also captured in the concepts of the maternal, nanny or pedagogical state (Pykett 2010, 2012). These descriptions illustrate how current governmental initiatives can be seen as saturated with a certain pedagogy, that is, 'soft or libertarian paternalist forms of governing' which draw on gendered perceptions of the encounter between welfare workers and citizens (Pykett 2012: 219). Soft paternalism implies a particular mode of governing that draws on norms of empathy, responsiveness and compassion while making certain choices available to the citizens in their decision-making process of how to resolve their situation. It is soft paternalism (and soft power) because 'choices are not blocked, fenced off, or significantly burdened ... [soft paternalism implies] a distinctive settlement between state and citizen focused on new cultural practices of governing explicitly through behaviour change' (Pykett 2012: 217).

By using concepts such as the maternal state, the pedagogical state, soft paternalism and even the nanny state, Pykett (2012) wants to emphasise the gendered nature of what she regards as a neoliberal threat to the welfare state (which partially explains the overlap with some of the discussions on the influence of a market way of thinking). Through her work, she demonstrates how the welfare state can be portrayed as maternal and nurturing but ultimately – and negatively – as a nanny state (Pykett 2012: 231). Rather than viewing the power of the state as a hard type of power with emphasis on (the bureaucracy's) hierarchy and formal authority, Pykett suggests investigating the softer 3-D and 4-D aspects of power, or how male and female interests are discursively constituted (but not necessarily determined) through local practices such as welfare work (Pykett 2012: 232).

This interest in psychology and pedagogy has been described by certain scholars as a therapeutic (Ecclestone and Brunila 2015) or psychosocial (Stenner *et al.* 2008: 411) turn in the ways in which (non-psychological) welfare issues are being dealt with in present-day societies. Dominant norms from the fields of psychology and pedagogy – such as empathy and compassion – thus lead to particular perceptions of citizens and their problems, which may cause an overemphasis on citizens' psychosocial vulnerabilities (Mik-Meyer 2004; Ecclestone and Brunila 2015). When scholars claim to have identified a so-called psychologisation or therapisation of welfare work, they seek to draw attention to the importance of discursive powers when investigating the roles of (psychological) norms in policy and in encounters between staff and citizens (Ecclestone and Brunila 2015: 487–488), not least because these norms frame certain dispositions of agents as relevant and others as not. However, as these scholars argue, a psychological context assumes a particular type of human subject, namely, someone who is capable of entering an empathic and compassionate relationship with the welfare worker and who perceives his or her situation in ways that correspond with these norms. Therefore, the pedagogical or psychological turn may create a particular sense of agency in both citizens and welfare workers, as well as requiring a particular habitus from the encountering parties. The risks hereof are that citizens may become too preoccupied with their own interests and psychological well-being and the welfare staff may become too engaged with the plethora of problems they inevitably have to solve due to the paternalistic tradition of their professions (Dean 2003: 696, 703). Moreover, the turn towards psychology may also be perceived as an inherently condescending approach to the citizens, as they from this perspective are seen as individuals who are unaware of their own real interests and psychological needs. This kind of soft power – in which one party is positioned as the knowledgeable party who (presumably) knows what is best for the encountering partner – creates associations to the working class of communism (who were also believed not to know their best interests) and may as such be viewed as an anti-democratic approach to the citizen.

A therapeutic approach to the citizen

Thus, these current studies that investigate the integration of norms from psychology in welfare work take a critical position on the notion of an economically rational and calculating subject: a subject which is often conceptualised through the so-called economic man model, a hypothetical individual who acts economic rationally out of self-interest and with the aim of maximising personal utility. In contrast hereto, these critical scholars draw attention to the 'irrational constitution of human life' (Isin 2004; Jones *et al.* 2013: 1; Haydock 2014) or rather the situated and environmentally bound rationality of human encounters. According to Jones and colleagues (2013), there are thus several serious limitations to the (economic) rationality assumption in much welfare work, as it takes the individual as its starting point instead of the environments in which the individual – and his or her 'free choice' – is always part (Jones *et al.* 2013: 16). Individuals are, in other words, always dealing with what can be called relational politics, that is, social categories which are '*lived out* ... in the everyday policy process [and which act] to reconfigure that very process itself' (Hunter 2012: 5 – emphasis in the original).

Jones and colleagues (2013) call for an ethical and political critique of three central aspects within the current so-called libertarian paternalism of present UK behavioural policies: 'Nudge, Think and Steer' (Jones *et al.* 2013: 163). These three concepts imply that the goal (of welfare workers) is to correct citizen behaviour by *nudging* them and making them *think* about their situation in an effort to *steer* them in the right direction. However, these authors suggest a fourth approach: 'Punch! [which] like a sudden self-imposed slap in the face ... reminds us to remain theoretically sensitive to power ... [as there is no such thing as] tactics of governance which purport to be politically neutral' (Jones *et al.* 2013: 164). With direct influence from Foucault, they argue that the actions expressed in encounters between welfare workers and citizens are governed and shaped by the disciplines of psychology, statistics and economics (Jones *et al.* 2013: 167). By suggesting the punch approach, they argue that any change in citizen behaviour – even when supposedly grounded in the citizen's own well-being – is profoundly political and not just of a technical nature, as any approach to behaviour change stems from carefully selected criteria by which the actions of individuals are measured and by which decisions about how to solve a particular (social) problem are made (Jones *et al.* 2013: 191).

A spatial power (Jones *et al.* 2010: 484) is always present and is embedded in the principles and norms of the environment (3-D), which through 'education, persuasion, inducement, management, incitement, motivation and encouragement' create social subjects (4-D) (Rose and Miller 2010: 274; Haugaard 2012). However, and instead of using the concept of irrationality to grasp these processes by which human behaviour is changed (Jones *et al.* 2013: 1; Haydock 2014), Rose and Miller (2010: 281) suggest the concept of political rationalities, as they believe that the work conducted in current welfare states is primarily governed by political decisions of what constitutes a good life, rather than technical calculations (Rose and Miller 2010: 294). When a therapeutic approach to the citizen becomes popular nowadays, it may then be because of political convictions and not (just) objective technical knowledge.

The therapeutic approach moreover involves emotional government (Sementelli 2006: 97), which places the welfare worker in the role of a therapist, a position which is not legitimised through law or political authority, as is the case with the administrators of the bureaucracy. The authority of a therapist is based on his or her training as an empathic and responsive person within the fields of psychology, counselling or psychiatry and thus relies on the perceived expertise of these disciplines (Sementelli 2006: 93). However, and in regards to the responsibility of citizens (a highly praised norm within present-day welfare work), a therapeutic approach may actually – although perhaps unintentionally – undermine this esteemed norm of modern societies, as the encounter between therapists and patients may also be about social control and domination. This encounter may, in other words, not accurately reflect the current valuation of responsibility, which implies that agents have freedom of (non-contextualised) will (Sementelli 2006: 100). From the perspective of Sementelli (2006: 111), a therapeutic approach to government therefore runs the risk of fundamentally changing the administrative state, not least because the therapeutic approach assumes that individual well-being is an individual rather than a social or relational phenomenon (Bondi 2005: 498).

The good citizen

The article 'Framing the Good Citizen' by Pykett and colleagues (2010) points to the political struggle that occurs when actors attempt to define and frame what it means (and requires) to be perceived as a good citizen today. This struggle occurs when citizens act and negotiate statuses and virtues and can therefore be studied by applying a performativity approach (or a symbolic interactionist approach) which enables the investigation of how people – in the roles of both therapist and patients – convert to and play the roles offered to them (Pykett *et al.* 2010: 533). This political struggle implies the recognition of authority as 'good citizens are made, not born ... in and by, the image of key actors' (Pykett *et al.* 2010: 532). This image is affected by the so-called psychosocial welfare state, that is, work in which '"psycho" resonates as surely as the "social" alongside the idea of "welfare"' (Stenner *et al.* 2008: 416). Welfare work has, to some extent, always included a psychological dimension, for instance, when staff are empathetic and help citizens achieve a sense of well-being through employment, education or social inclusion (Stenner *et al.* 2008: 433). Being well and receiving welfare are thus two interdependent phenomena which produce a particular type of relationship between laypeople, the political and (what at a given time in history is perceived as) expertise (Ferguson 2001: 42). The argument is thus that the self is a reflexive project in which the question '"who shall I be?" is inextricably bound up with "how shall I live?"' (Ferguson 2001: 50), which is a fundamentally political and moral undertaking. Consequently, present-day welfare work is not only regarded as addressing and resolving important issues (such as abuse or violence) but it is also perceived as work that invites and enables citizens to 'explore who they are and how they should live' (Ferguson 2001: 53).

Psycho-policies (Friedli and Stearn 2015) that focus on the right attitude to, for instance, employment, initiate a moral project within the unemployed instead of focusing on the structural aspects, which prevent certain individuals from gaining employment. These kinds of psycho-policies may actually stigmatise vulnerable citizens and individuals with few financial and reflexive resources (Friedli and Stearn 2015: 44–45). The point is that the situations and behaviours of unemployed people are often perceived and intrepreted without regard for context, history, political struggles or how norms from psychology affect evaluations of responsible behaviour and what it means to be a good citizen today. The issue of unemployment is therefore in danger of becoming psychologised and pathologised at the micro level and thereby of changing the focus from economic strategies and financial redistribution to the 'moral imagination of policy makers, politicians and service providers' (McDonald *et al.* 2003: 520; McDonald and Marston 2005). Because the pedagogical authority automatically centres around the attitudes, motivations, responsiveness and deficits of the unemployed, this type of authority will always run the risk of infantilising the welfare client (McDonald and Marston 2005: 387).

As the discussions have shown so far, much criticism is aimed at welfare work which centres around the psychological and pedagogical norms of empathy, compassion and responsiveness. The following section will take a closer look at the concepts of personalisation and co-production, as these approaches are prioritised by welfare workers and are linked to the psychologisation of welfare work as well.

Personalisation and co-production

The criminal justice system is set up to degrade, disempower, depersonalise. ...
The personalisation agenda is set up to do the opposite. It is very hard to assert
yourself as an individual in that system. We've got a lot of unpicking to do to
achieve that – among prison officers, but also the legal professions. (Staff at
Ministry of Justice, UK, cited in Needham 2011: 42)

In the UK especially, the newly arisen focus on a personalisation approach
to the citizen has been eagerly discussed (e.g., Leadbetter and Lownsbrough
2005; Barnes 2011; Mladenov *et al.* 2015; Needham and Glasby 2015), not
least because far from all welfare areas are well suited for this approach, as
the quote illustrates. Some scholars argue that welfare states are currently
transitioning from a uniform to a personalised welfare state (Cutler *et al.*
2007: 851), a transition that can be regarded as either a 'radical revolu-
tion' aimed at securing a person-centred approach to welfare work or an
attempt to 'roll back the boundaries of the welfare state' and hence – first
and foremost – save money. 'Personalization is either the best thing since
sliced bread or the end of the welfare state as we know it', as Needham and
Glasby (2014: 5) put it. According to Needham (2011b), who is one of the
principal scholars on personalisation, this new person-centred approach
seeks to reflect the ways in which people live their lives, rather than arti-
ficial departmental boundaries of how problems (and people) should be
categorised. She argues that the personalisation approach is applicable to
everyone (not only citizens with social care needs), that it places people
in the roles of experts in their own lives and that the approach has been
shown to reduce welfare costs (Needham 2011b: 57–59).

Personalisation is part of a putting people first agenda and may be
viewed as a way of strengthening the ties between citizenship and community. It may therefore come as no surprise that the concept was particularly
prevalent during New Labour's final year as head of the UK government.
The concept of personalisation was presented alongside related concepts,
such as tailored and individualised services (Needham 2011a: 1), which
refer to a similar approach in which welfare workers tailor their work to fit
the needs of the individual citizen and, in doing so, detach the welfare work
from the (bureaucratic and financial) interests of the welfare staff and its
managers. Needham (2011a: 4) explains,

Personalisation was a term that helped to summarise all that was perceived to
be wrong with existing public services and all that could be done to improve
them. ... So powerful and authentic were these stories, so full of win-wins –
more satisfied service users, more fulfilled staff, lower costs, reduced depend-
ence on the state – that it seemed impossible to challenge them, except as an
apologist for an unsatisfactory status quo. (Needham 2011a: 4)

However, the personalisation approach also reveals certain ambiguities: when welfare workers take this approach to the citizens and their problems, then both citizens and welfare workers must assume new roles and positions. Citizens need to take charge of their lives and problems, and welfare workers must ensure that this is done (Needham 2011a: 87). The professional expertise of the welfare workers must, in other words, give way to the informal knowledge of citizens and their (possibly different) perceptions of their problem and its causes, as the knowledge of citizens is of paramount importance to the personalisation approach (Needham 2011a: 94, 137).

This change in expertise challenges the hitherto privileged status of welfare workers, which may cause resistance to the personalisation agenda. Staff's ambiguous position within the personalisation agenda has, for instance, been pointed out by social workers who, on the one hand, are reluctant to relinquish control and, on the other hand, readily assume the roles of the productive collaborators in pursuit of securing the person-centred qualities in their work (Needham 2011a: 145, 154). The ambiguous position of welfare workers also relates to the goal of making citizens responsible, as not all citizens have the – in the eyes of the welfare workers – correct knowledge or grasp of their situation and may consequently be unable to act in a correct and responsible manner.

When the personalisation approach rejects and disregards the (common and widely agreed upon) notion of information asymmetry between the professional (expert) welfare worker and the (ignorant) citizen – a notion which traditionally has been the basis for the exercise of professional power – then problems similar to the ones discussed in Chapter 6 arise: firstly, in relation to vulnerable groups who are incapable of assuming the knowledge position given to them by the personalisation agenda or who are perceived as in need of sanctions and constraints (e.g., criminals and unemployed people who are perceived as lazy) (see also Ferguson 2007), and secondly, in relation to welfare work in areas in which professional expertise remains dominant (Needham 2011b). However, the popularity of the personalisation approach within, for instance, social work may be related to key ambitions of this work, as suggested by Ferguson (2007: 389), namely, the rejection of paternalism within social services and the wish to give voice to all citizens, to put them first and make them responsible for their own situations. It is an ambition that steers social work away from its previous focus on the structural aspects of citizens' problems. In embracing the personalisation approach, social work no longer centres around what citizens can expect from the state but instead how 'the citizen *should be* – in this case, active, responsible and enterprising' (Scourfield 2007: 112 – emphasis in the original).

Within the field of education, Pykett (2009) discusses how homeschooling (or de-schooling, as she writes) is an example of a personalisation approach to children, which – on a positive note – may help them develop the abilities to make choices, take responsibility for their learning and become flexible independent individuals. However, as Pykett (2009) and other critical educational scholars point out, the focus on individual choice and responsibility embedded within the personalisation agenda shows an alarming resemblance to what is critically described as neoliberalism and the valuation of free-market thinking (Pykett 2009: 384). In its ideal form, the focus of the personalisation approach on choice is not (only) about decision-making as understood from free-market thinking; it is also about a weakening responsibility of the state.

Thus, a paradox begins to take form regarding the personalisation approach, as it can be perceived as a technology of neoliberalism aimed at rolling back the welfare state. From another perspective, however, personalisation is an approach that seeks to deliver tailored (and thus probably more costly) person-centred help to clients and patients of the welfare state. Regardless of which interpretation you favour, the personalisation approach is undoubtedly one that perceives and urges citizens of all ages to become 'innovative, self-motivated, responsible, entrepreneurial and creative persons ... [who can] express their choices, flexibility and needs through their own "authentic" consumer world' (Pykett 2009: 385, 387), a description that greatly resembles the ideal citizen of the market context. However, and of great importance here, there does not seem to be much resemblance to the ideal citizen of the bureaucracy, as the personalisation approach actively and explicitly distances itself from bureaucratic and technocratic ways of conducting welfare work. As put by Lloyd (2010: 195), 'in social work, the personalisation agenda is perceived to offer an opportunity to re-establish core social work norms by shedding the heavily bureaucratic administrative approach that has dominated community care services'.

Even though it may prove a difficult task to be genuinely critical towards an approach that seeks to improve the match between welfare users and services, increase cost-effectiveness, boost welfare efficiency and give citizens primary power in the management of their own affairs, one can easily oversell personalisation (Spicker 2013: 1262, 1265). In reviewing and addressing each of these arguments (which mainly arise from linking the personalisation approach to market mechanisms), Spicker (2013) finds that although these positive arguments do bear some weight, it may be difficult in certain cases to see what a personalisation approach can actually contribute with (Spicker 2013: 1269), especially when considering welfare areas characterised by choice constraints and/or scarce financial resources. Moreover, personalisation may cause a so-called de-professionalisation of welfare work due to its ambition to position citizens as experts of their own lives (and problems) at the expense of professional expertise (Ferguson 2007: 400).

Co-production is another way of conceptualising the ambition of improving the quality of public services and the encounter between welfare workers and citizens. Co-production is about including citizens and community organisations in welfare work, both in the design and production of public services and in the ways in which citizens consume and benefit from these services (Needham 2008: 221; Durose and Richardson 2016). The focus on design is a way to emphasise the importance of placing the citizens at the centre of welfare work and to extract and harness their opinions of their needs and situations, just as users are placed at the centre of commercial design (Durose and Richardson 2016: 4). Thus, in an effort to engage with citizens and enter into co-production relationships with them, welfare workers must establish a dialogue with the citizens and not merely seek out information about their situations, as such information and the search hereof will necessarily be framed and directed by the expertise of the welfare workers. Instead and within the frame of co-production, citizens and welfare workers are positioned as people who ought to listen to each other. In the words of Needham,

> co-production can be a therapeutic tool (building trust and communication between participants, allowing bureaucrats and citizens to explain their perspective and listen to others) as well as a diagnostic one (revealing citizens' needs, identifying the main causes of delivery problems and negotiating effective means to resolve them). (2008: 223)

Co-production entails – and ideally fosters – long-term relationships between welfare workers and citizens, a relationship in which both parties engage in dialogue (Bovaird 2007: 847). However, and similar to much of the cited work on psychology-inspired welfare that aims to put the citizen first, this goal may not be easy to achieve.

Concluding comments: the role of agency in a psychological context

Psychology-inspired welfare work – including the personalisation and co-production approaches to the citizen – has received much criticism. Firstly, the focus of the approach on the citizen's ability to receive empathy and compassion and to be responsive and responsible for his or her situation (and thus the securement of citizen agency as in the market context) may result in the downplaying of the responsibilities of the state (Durose and Richardson 2016: 36). Within many policy areas, the problems of citizens are complex, 'wicked' and 'squishy' (Durose and Richardson 2016: 49) and cannot be resolved by the responsibilisation of the citizen alone, but need to involve government as well as professionals and their expertise (and responsibility).

Secondly, the reallocation of expertise within this approach from welfare workers onto citizens can be regarded as an expression of soft power, as this process subtly points to the informal rules of the welfare encounter. Even though one can argue that expertise is 'something people do rather than something people have or hold' (Carr 2010: 18–19), and hence is an interactional rather than possessive phenomenon, expertise also entails the organisation of knowledge and is therefore framed in a particular norm-based way in institutional environments. Thus, the expertise of staff working in organisations which emphasise bureaucratic principles is quite different from the expertise of staff working in organisations which emphasise market values, as well as the expertise related to organisational work influenced by norms of empathy, compassion and putting the citizen first (Bartels 2013: 472). Given that the context of the welfare encounter is – hypothetically and for the sake of argument – about coaching the citizens, then the agency of both welfare workers and citizens may never rise above a first-order agency. Citizens and welfare workers may be able to adjust the expectations of the encountering party (first order) but will fail to change the overarching agenda of the encounter in any profound ways (if it, for instance, is chaired by a coach) (second order of agency) and must therefore accept the roles or positions of coaches and coachees.

Thirdly, the influence of psychology leads to an individualisation of social problems, which rather than being viewed as, in fact, *social* problems will then be approached through an individualistic lens and sought to be resolved by addressing the motivation of the unemployed citizen or by instilling a positive spirit within, for instance, the homeless. Again, the argument is that the context of the welfare work – be it the principles of the bureaucracy, values of the market or norms from psychology – must be regarded as a form of soft power that has a tremendous impact on both encountering parties, as these contexts strongly affect which actions can be considered rational and meaningful and which cannot. Their impact also rests on the fact that most often these three contexts exist simultaneously, which makes the rules, principles and norms of the situated interaction even more difficult for the participating parties to grasp.

Lastly, the idea of a power-free relation between welfare workers (in the role of facilitators, coaches, etc., who only wish the best for citizens) and citizens (in the role of experts, coachees, etc., who ought to voice their opinions) may moreover cloud or distort the relationship, as the rules and demands of the welfare state are essential features of the encounter and are arguably quite different from the power-free and neutral encounter in a coaching session (in which the coachee, by the way, may leave whenever he or she wants).

In summary, the agency of both citizens and welfare workers is not only related to the bureaucratic rules and procedures, or the marketisation efforts within welfare work. The agency of citizens and welfare workers is also related to a psychologisation of welfare work, which automatically places the welfare worker in the role of facilitator, therapist and coach and the citizen as a responsive individual with expert knowledge about his or her own situation; roles which, in turn, render personalisation and co-production strategies as the 'obvious' approaches in the welfare encounter. However, the psychologisation of welfare work also implies that citizens are in need of empathy, compassion and other types of (personal) help from facilitators, coaches or even therapists. This implication may result in what some scholars have termed the infantilisation of citizens, as the citizen is then automatically assumed as in need of help and (parental) care. Just as welfare workers may experience problems with their traditional expert role, citizens may also struggle with two inherently contradicting roles: that of the (supposed) expert in the welfare encounter and that of the help-seeking individual. A therapeutic approach to welfare work centres the citizen (e.g., by giving voice to the citizen) while simultaneously placing the individual as in need of care and help. Furthermore, a therapeutic approach does not emphasise the collective, which is why this approach also marks a move away from a political understanding of democracy (as a collective decision-making process) towards a therapeutic perspective concerned with the subjective views of individuals (Chandler 2000: 11).

Part III

Welfare encounters in practice

8

The power of bureaucracy, market and psychology in citizen–staff encounters

Introduction

This chapter addresses how the principles of bureaucracy, values of the market and norms from psychology influence welfare encounters in practice. As discussed, sociologists have for many years shown great interest in the ways in which categorisation practices among practitioners produce institutional identities, such as 'the afflicted', 'the deadlocked' and 'the flexible' (Gubrium and Holstein 2001; Mik-Meyer 2004). The goal of this research has been to examine how these institutionally anchored categories affect the perception of the individuals who encounter the welfare state, as well as the individuals' own perceptions of their situation. In Bourdieusian terms, the goal is to show how the different (symbolic) capitals of a particular welfare field affect the perceptions and actions of agents (Bourdieu 1998). The concept of interactive categories (Hacking 1999) illustrates that categorisations of people – and how they diagnose and categorise themselves – change their self-perceptions, as well as the ways in which their encountering party perceives them. Diagnoses and other types of social categories are thus bound to the historical period and particular context in which they are created. They are, as such, social phenomena which reflect dominant perceptions of what it takes to be perceived as in need of help or self-reliant, ill or well, normal or abnormal and so forth (Foucault 1987; Hacking 1999). Becker (1997) and Goffman (1990a) address, for instance, the matter of social diagnoses, with particular attention to the negative effects these categorisations have on the people who receive them. By drawing on forensic studies, Becker developed the labelling theory, in which labels are related to dominant norms in society. Goffman had similar ambitions when developing his theory on stigma, as the primary aim hereof was to show how the perception of a stigma must be seen as embedded within the dominant norms of a particular society and point in time (in relation to disability, see Mik-Meyer 2015a, 2016a, 2016b).

Thus, when present-day Western societies witness an increase in, for instance, clinical depression – which, for laypeople, is typically associated with passive, inhibited and functionally inadequate persons – then this development may be related to the fact that these societies praise values and principles stemming from both the market and psychology, such as the citizen's ability to be responsive to empathy and compassion, proactive, responsible and choice-making, more so now than ever before. Diagnoses such as depression and stress are, in other words, not only descriptors of the particular person and his or her medical or social situation; they also shed light on a current battle between particular rationales of (in this case) a welfare field and a health field (Bourdieu and Wacquant 1996). Diagnoses thus reflect dominant rationales in a society – such as the Danish, from which the analyses of this present chapter are drawn – about which behaviours and states one should regard as abnormal or ill.

Additionally, there is today an increasing number of citizens who report and complain about pains which cannot be diagnosed (Mik-Meyer and Johansen 2009). Within the scholarly literature, such people fall into the category of persons with medically unexplained symptoms (MUS), which is yet another category or diagnosis that is open to criticism (Jutel 2010). This description includes people who (among other things) experience pains in one or several parts of the body, but where the medical professionals are unable to detect the source or cause of the pain. In certain contexts (and points of time), such people are described by diagnoses such as fibromyalgia or whiplash, while in others, they are identified as chronic pain patients, mentally unstable, stress or depression stricken or even hysterical. The names are many, but their multitude does not render them any less important because the labels assigned to the pains and symptoms indicate whether the person is perceived as credible (Mik-Meyer 2011), whether the person is perceived as legitimately ill or someone who 'merely' suffers from a weak psyche (Mik-Meyer and Obling 2012). For instance, in many contexts the diagnosis of fibromyalgia entails the assumption that, more than anything else, the person suffers from a weak mental constitution, which in turn means that the citizen's descriptions of physical pain are often dismissed as medically invalid. This diagnosis thus gives rise to suspicion because if a person is deemed untrustworthy in this important regard, then how can he or she be trusted when it comes to other problematic aspects of his or her life?

As such, diagnoses and other classification tools can be seen as powerful for a number of reasons. Firstly, they allow the citizen to describe and explain his or her complaints in a way which the surroundings (e.g., a spouse, workplace or welfare organisation) can accept. Secondly, they often allow the citizen – even for the briefest of time – to be supported and provided for by the public system. Thirdly, they reflect certain (contextually and temporally) dominant perceptions of health and illness and give certain individuals – possessing a certain kind of habitus – access to field-specific resources, which may help them reach their desired end. Fourthly, they draw attention to certain characteristics which the citizen is assumed to have, given his or her diagnosis. A depressed person is, for instance, expected to behave in a certain way and may even be assumed to have a particular (divergent) personality.

However, it is important to note that when diagnoses are referred to as social constructions, this is not the same as disputing the existence of the symptoms captured by these diagnoses. The symptoms may exist and the pains may occur. The point is that diagnoses are much more than merely the names of functional problems in the mental and physical body. Diagnoses reflect a larger social environment (Hall 1997) – 2-D, 3-D and 4-D powers – and produce particular expectations of how citizens (and welfare workers) ought to behave in different contexts. The ways in which society categorises symptoms or social troubles affect the expectations of welfare workers as well (Gubrium and Järvinen 2014b; Mik-Meyer and Villadsen 2014). Welfare workers are, for instance, today engaged in caring, comforting and rule-abiding relations, as well as documenting and servicing citizens.

However, amid the hustle and bustle of everyday life most welfare workers probably forget that the categories and diagnoses they use in their work actively produce a particular image of the person described by these categories, an image which relates to characteristics other than those described by the medical descriptors of the diagnosis. Diagnoses and other categorisation tools thus create a new way of perceiving and understanding (the actions of) a person, which also defines the way in which welfare staff ought to respond. As mentioned, the professional backgrounds and habitus of the welfare staff cause them to employ certain social categories and diagnoses when trying to solve the problems of citizens. However, this is not the only influence on the categorisation process, as the ways in which public organisations conduct welfare work – for instance, the choice of which particular professions to employ in an effort to solve a given problem or the general organisation of the welfare work – greatly impact daily categorisation processes as well (Mik-Meyer 2004). Moreover, the dominant principles and norms of powerful actors (individuals and institutions) constitute the doxa of a field and thus affect which diagnoses are perceived as meaningful and legitimate.

As the following two cases will illustrate, the emphasis on bureaucratic principles, market values, NPM techniques and norms from psychology differ according to both the welfare area and the particular encounter. Bureaucratic principles and NPM may affect the welfare areas of employment and health more than, for instance, the welfare area of social work. Similarly, social work may be more influenced by norms from psychology than other welfare areas. The first case illustrates the influence of legislation, adherence to regulation and other principles related to the field of bureaucracy, as well as the effects of individualising stories of stress and depression, a focus which relates to both market values and norms from psychology. The second case shows how discretionary practices are played out in social work and demonstrates in great detail how discretion relates to the rules and procedures of the bureaucracy, as well as to (psychological) approaches of empathy, compassion, co-production and personalisation.

Powerful negotiations of stress and depression

The currently expanding group of citizens who experience stress, depression and other (at times) medically unexplained symptoms is relevant for the argument of this book, as the troubles of this citizen group illustrate that the welfare worker's job is also to act as moral entrepreneur (Becker 1997) when encountering citizens. The question which doctors and caseworkers, as well as politicians and other debaters, seek to answer is whether these citizens are legitimately ill despite their lack of a biomedical diagnosis. The first case shows how doctors (the GPs and municipal medical consultants), caseworkers and citizens negotiate the diagnoses of stress and depression (see also Mik-Meyer and Johansen 2009; Mik-Meyer 2010a, 2011; Mik-Meyer and Obling 2012).[1]

The research project reported from here found that the legal demands for documentation, the financial context of the welfare work and dominant norms regarding work ethics, perceptions of legitimate illnesses and so forth were all key aspects of the analysis. The study furthermore found that citizens with MUS challenged the roles of both doctors and caseworkers, as it was difficult to act as a doctor or caseworker when the complaints of the opposing party – the citizen – could not be documented by using the tools of biomedicine. The main task of the doctors and caseworkers was therefore to make a moral judgement of whether they found the citizen to be trustworthy and credible. This extension of their professional work can be seen as connected to the increasingly detailed steering of NPM within the social sector, which means that citizens ideally must have a biomedically confirmed diagnosis if they are to become eligible for sickness benefits. The legitimacy of this group of people as ill consequently depends on the GP's ability to create an explanatory framework that can be used when assessing the symptoms and condition of a patient, even in cases where a biomedical diagnosis is absent (Cassell 2004). These citizens thus challenge both the traditional biomedical approach of doctors (the field of medicine and its particular capitals), and the bureaucratic procedures of the social system, which demand that caseworkers document the symptoms of a citizen.

The negotiation of stress and depression

Categorisation practices related to stress and depression are relevant, as these (often vague and ambiguous) diagnoses are becoming increasingly prevalent in Western societies, including Denmark. Even though it was unclear for the study participants which symptoms or conditions would qualify for the diagnosis of stress or depression, these diagnoses were predominantly given to women and less-educated persons in their forties and fifties (Mik-Meyer and Johansen 2009; Mik-Meyer 2011). However, this chapter centres on other structural factors: the doxa of the different fields, that is, the effect of various forms of capitals and rationales on how to evaluate legitimate illnesses. According to the study's participating doctors and caseworkers, the diagnoses of stress and depression (which were given to two-thirds of the participating citizens) had become much more frequent than, for instance, five years earlier. Stress and depression were diagnoses which were often brought into play when talking about what it meant to be busy or ill. Here, a caseworker challenges the connection between stress and a (too) busy work life:

> Sometimes we are sitting with people who are stressed, right? And they describe what kinds of work or tasks that caused their stress and you think to yourself, 'Join the club!' I realise that it might sound a bit cynical, but I just think that I would never call in sick because of such things. If that was the case, I could have taken a sick leave many years ago, you know? Because of stress. So what levels are we talking about here? Everyone's limits are different, and the people we have here at this job centre, their limitations are very low. That's just how it is.

It may come as no surprise that the participating citizens, who were on sick leave due to stress, did not share this opinion. They typically identified problematic work relations as the cause for their stress, work relations which resulted from, for instance, increasing work pressures, managers who were indifferent to their attempts to set boundaries, prolonged increasing workloads (which at a certain point became unsustainable) and so on.

The ambiguity of how to define stress revealed two important parameters against which stories of stress were measured: the perception of the citizens' trustworthiness and the perception of acceptable workloads and social relations at work. The evaluation of stress was, in other words, primarily done according to parameters that lay beyond medical rationalisation and were consequently guided by things other than medical expertise. The caseworkers – who in this study generally believed that the concept of stress mostly implied lazy, untrustworthy citizens who actually were just normally busy – explained that these citizens simply had to 'pull themselves together'. However, this morally guided rationality was rarely shared by the doctors who encountered the citizens in their clinics. The GPs often shared another politicised belief, namely, that stress actually could be caused by too demanding work conditions. They even talked about how modern society was to blame for the increasing number of citizens falling ill with stress. As a doctor explained, 'I believe that the increase in stress is caused by society. Well, its sounds very political, but that's how I see it. It's an increasing tendency, and in many cases, the stress is caused by people's work conditions'.

Between the two opposite but clearly defined ways of perceiving stress – as either an illegitimate illness of people with (normal) busy work lives or a legitimate illness caused by unsustainably demanding work conditions – was a large grey area in which other perceptions of stress were found, perceptions which also related to current dominant norms in society. Within this grey area, stress was, for instance, a symptom or expression of a crisis within the person's life: 'We try to engage with these people rather quickly because we think, "What's the matter here?" Stress can be any number of things, so it's important to uncover it', a caseworker explained when answering a question of how she would respond when becoming informed about a stress-related case. Her colleague (a caseworker as well) expanded on this psychologically informed rationality: 'What is the cause of the stress? It can be so many things. It can be work, but it can also be things at home that cause the stress to take hold. Remodelling the house, getting a divorce, children who are having problems and so on'.

Additionally, 'psychosocial problems' or 'life pains' were expressions used by many caseworkers to describe conditions which were believed to lie just beneath the surface of sick leave due to stress. From this perspective, stress was neither busyness nor illness, but rather a catch-all category for various psychosocial problems, such as poorly managed life crises. Thus, if the illnesses of citizens were labelled as stress, the citizens would then be approached and regarded as clients (and not patients) and as such 'much easier to deal with', as a caseworker explained. In these cases, the problems of citizens were based in the field of psychology and citizens were therefore automatically perceived as in need of coaching and guidance in how to manage their work and life situations better, which, in turn, placed the responsibility for recovery on the citizen. In many cases, the client would receive offers such as sessions with a stress coach in an effort to better facilitate 'the process of healing', as a caseworker said. This psychosocial perception of stress was further supported by a doctor, who explained, 'It comes and goes with trends and fashions. A few years ago, these people weren't ill with stress. They had whiplash and then they had back pains and now they suffer from stress'. In his opinion, stress was a concept that described psychological troubles which were previously defined by categories such as whiplash and back pains. This perspective was also supported by caseworkers who talked about the decrease in fibromyalgia cases and a simultaneous increase in stress-related cases.

This change in concepts within a Danish context probably also relates to the fact that the only hospital department in Denmark that diagnosed fibromyalgia was actually the target of general mistrust from doctors in regards to this very diagnosis. For this and similar reasons, more and more Danish municipalities have employed doctors (medical consultants) who function as translators of both medical documents produced in hospital departments such as the fibromyalgia centre and (politicised) documents by the citizens' GPs. Similar to their other municipal colleagues, the medical consultants typically take a very cost-effective and conservative approach to evaluating the medical reports of citizens. They often transform vague medical descriptions into social problems and consequently lower the costs for the social system: sickness benefits are, for instance, much higher than social benefits and are given independently of spousal income.

Even though the participating doctors did write somewhat alternative medical notes about their patients, with emphasis on, for instance, a strenuous workload, these alternative medical evaluations were mostly rejected by the municipal medical consultants. In addition to having a (cost-effective, conservative) biomedical view of how to measure and evaluate symptoms, they had to follow the rules and procedures of the social system, a system which in Denmark leaves very little room for supporting these somewhat alternative medical evaluations. Even though the municipal medical consultants were never in contact with the citizens, their opinions were nonetheless highly regarded by the municipal caseworker. The documents of the medical consultants were simply believed to be more 'objective', as several caseworkers explained. This presumed objectivity may relate to the fact that the work of the medical consultants was rid of human contact, and thereby personal interaction as well. The following interview excerpt illustrates how a municipal medical consultant evalutates the symptoms of a citizens; an evaluation that is based on the citizens medical journal. This particular medical consultant begins by answering the question of how he would describe his job:

> Medical consultant: It's about coming to a decision on the illness-related information of the case. That's basically it. And then the next step is whether or not there is a 'documented health-related impairment', as it's called for

legal reasons. We are not allowed to evaluate their ability to work. As soon as the case reaches my desk it is called 'documented health-related impairment'. Whether or not there is a documented health-related impairment, whether it is temporary or chronic, whether or not we can recommend the gathering of additional information and, of course, if there are any treatment options that haven't yet been utilised.

Interviewer: And you make these evaluations based on the journals you receive?

Medical consultant: Based on the paperwork, yes.

Interviewer: So, paper-patients in a sense?

Medical consultant: In a sense, yes. It's not patients, it is something else. But yes, we evaluate the cases based on the paperwork and we are not allowed to contact the citizen.

Interviewer: You are not allowed to contact the citizen?

Medical consultant: No. That part lies with the caseworkers. [...]

Interviewer: Okay. If we consider the group of people on long-term sick leave, those with vague illnesses, who are they? Can you make any general statements about this group?

Medical consultant: [*Coughs and mumbles to himself and into the paper*] What is this? Oh. I can't say anything generally about that. Long-term sick leave. Well, you are the one who defines vague illnesses. I don't really know how.... It's not written anywhere in my book.

Interviewer: What if we call them functional impairments [*a medical term*] instead?

Medical consultant: Well, that is a massive problem, and if you intend to approach this topic, it'll require a great ... it demands a lot of effort. Functional impairments are very strange.... Many disorders stem from bad functionality or something similar, and then they become functional impairments. But they have also morphed into something else, something that isn't actually there, you know, and that's a whole different conversation. So, the concept of functional impairments is for me very undefined. Bam bam bam.... It is nothing but ... what's it called? When you invent diseases and there are no real bases for the disease? So, I have no way of evaluating these types of illnesses, I can only make decisions about things that are documented. Things that are written.

Interviewer: But the group of people whom others would call patients or citizens with functional impairments, would you call them anything?

Medical consultant: No.

Interviewer: Do you consider them a group?

Medical consultant: No, I do not. Well, I am still a bit unsure about what other people mean when they talk about functional impairments because it is a very ambiguous concept and, frankly, a very difficult one for me to perceive. But we could of course define the concept by discussing the one you're talking about. Because I get a really large number of cases, of people who in my opinion aren't sick at all, you know? Of course, they have some ailments and they complain a lot, that's true.

This dialogue shows how the procedures of the social system – that is, evaluating medical reports rather than flesh and blood patients and only allowing a focus on biomedically documented illnesses, 'things that are written' – produce a particular evaluation of a citizen's health status. This evaluation is in stark contrast to the medical reports of the GPs, who encounter these citizens in their clinics and engage in what they call 'a more holistic evaluation' of their situation. This particular medical consultant quoted here cared neither for the categorisations made by the GP nor for the – in his eyes – vague pseudo medical term of functional impairments. His evaluation was rather based on an economic policy-centred rationality aiming at reducing the number of people given sickness benefits.

Another important finding of this study (which relates to the 2-D procedural and legislative frameworks of the encounter) was the prevalence of 3-D 'stress-related depression' diagnoses in many Danish municipalities. Within these municipalities, the GPs preferred this diagnosis because stress – in their eyes – was not perceived as an actual medical diagnosis by the medical consultants, as indicated in the dialogue extract. However, depression is a clinically acknowledged diagnosis with various established procedures for identification and treatment within the medical field. The category of stress-related depression thus became a way for the doctors to make their patients (and their symptoms) fit within the municipality's need for documentation of diagnoses (3-D and 4-D), rather than the other way around. If a citizen was described as suffering from stress-related depression, then the medical system would take over and the citizen would both be granted (the increased) sickness benefits and receive proper medical treatment (typically pharmaceutics supplemented by psychosocial therapy).

Similar to stress, the diagnosis of depression has increasingly become part of our everyday vocabulary, which in and of itself contributes to blurring the lines between being sad and being ill, and thus how to evaluate these symptoms. Depression can range from mild states of melancholy (which do not require treatment) to mid-level depressions (which require the patient to undergo psychosocial and medical treatment) to severe depressions (involving hospitalisation and thorough psychiatric treatment). In this particular study, the participating citizens were believed to suffer from milder forms of depression. This is the tipping point where sadness becomes illness; the contact face between the field of psychology and the field of medicine, as well as their different rationales. This problem of how to perceive the symptoms of

these citizens may explain why especially caseworkers described depression
in such negative terms.

Even though the diagnosis of depression would secure the much
preferred legal position as a legitimately ill person (with the accompany-
ing favourable economic compensation), many citizens were reluctant
towards this diagnosis. These citizens described a process of stigmati-
sation when people found out about their diagnosis as depressed. This
stigma could arise from their own perceptions and stories about the implications of being depressed, as well as from the perceptions and stories of
others. A participant explained how he felt embarrassed when having to
tell people that he had depression. He thought people would then 'start
thinking about psychiatric facilities and stuff like that. How sick are you,
why are you sick and are you actually crazy?', as he said. In a similar vein,
other participants appeared to accept the diagnosis but wanted to keep
it a private matter. Another person even compared admitting to having
depression with confessing to attending AA meetings: 'Hi, I'm Susanne
and I'm an alcoholic'. The rationality within the subfield of psychiatry (in
which depression belongs) imply that depression-stricken individuals both
have lost control and have a weak strength of character, characteristics
which are regarded as highly problematic by most Danes as they confront
dominant norms of being in control and having a strong personal character. Other participants were even more sceptical towards the diagnosis:
a woman, for instance downright refused to accept it. She did not want
to 'suffer from a mental illness', as she said. In her own opinion, she was
'burned out' and 'hypersensitive', not depressed. These various ways of
resisting and refusing the label of depression all seem to relate to 4-D
powers: to a wish of distancing oneself from the negative associations
related to depression. To be burned out or hypersensitive was, conversely,
a descriptor which related to a market rationale and its associated values
of efficiency, toughness and so on and did not negatively stigmatise the
carrier as a depression diagnosis would.

However, some participants did view the diagnosis of depression
through a positive lens. One woman explained that by getting this diagnosis, she became legitimately ill in the eyes of the caseworkers instead
of merely being someone who ought to just pull herself together. She had
no problems with the solution of medicine presented to her. She elaborated on the differences between the two diagnoses as follows: 'With
stress people think, "Uh, get a grip. You don't have any more work than I
do. Buck up". But if I have a stress-related depression and take medication
for it, then okay, I am actually sick'. Another participant accepted the
depression diagnosis as well and explained how she had 'browsed the
websites of the Psychiatry Foundation and the Association for Depression

many times and had read a lot about "what others do and how" and stuff like that. And it's actually been nice'. These websites helped her understand her situation and interpret her symptoms. The doctors were also well aware of these websites and their potential impact, and often took quite a critical stance towards the International Classification of Diseases (ICD10) (the biomedical protocol for diagnosing depression) criteria. As one doctor explained, such 'tests aren't the whole truth, you know. You have to look at people too'. He continued to reflect on the context of the diagnostic practices:

> But we use the test to have something tangible to act from. And we have to use it if we want to refer young people to a psychologist. It's a fairly new service that people can get financial help to psychological treatment of mild cases of depression. But, in order to get it, you need to show the results from an ICD10 test.

Even though a test may neither seem as valid or tangible as, for instance, a blood test (as mentioned by another doctor) nor suggest specific courses of treatment, the ICD10 test was nevertheless perceived with positivity and appreciation, not least because an affirmative score meant that the patient would be able to receive financial benefits. This test helped transform depression from merely a vague condition to an (apparently) objective and diagnosable illness. However, far from all caseworkers regarded such tests as useful due to their general perception of depression as primarily a psychosocial illness. These caseworkers believed that this particular group of citizens were difficult to help with medicine because their problems, in fact, were psychosocial. To these caseworkers, depression was a separate social problem which, of course, required a different (social) solution. The sadness and despair of citizens were believed to be caused by either external social conditions (typically work conditions) or internal mental or personality-related factors (such as a problematic childhood, marital issues, life crisis or burnout), and neither were thus regarded as solvable through medication. These caseworkers' dispositions thus aligned with a psychosocial way of rationalising, and their arguments could be reduced to neither a market and NPM rationale nor the rationalities of the medical field.

While a small proportion of the participating caseworkers referred to depression as a 'shotgun' diagnosis, the majority of them talked about how the doctors (in their opinion) used the diagnosis far too broadly and in an effort to make almost any symptom fit within its scope. According to these caseworkers, it was an easy fix to diagnose patients with depression and to prescribe antidepressants, which was why they regarded their own primary task as identifying the actual cause of the depression. However, this task was challenged by the 'boxes' of the social system, as explained by two caseworkers:

> Caseworker 1: You must be able to document that you are unable to work due to illness – your own illness, that is. And this documentation has to come from a doctor, and if the doctor decides to give the person another diagnosis, then what can we do? We can let the doctor know that someone is having a rough time, but then we enter the world of existential problems and you can't get a sick leave because of those.

> Caseworker 2: Unless they've led to a depression. Then it's possible to do something, but it's still difficult to get them to fit in those boxes.

According to these caseworkers, the problems of citizens were defined (only) by the diagnoses made by the doctors and the current legislation (the boxes of the social system): a person cannot be unable to work and eligible for sickness benefits due to existential (social) problems. However, if the problem of a citizen was defined by a biomedical diagnosis (the 'depression' box), then the person had a valid reason for taking sick leave – and, not to forget, receive sickness benefits.

Concluding comments

This case on depression and stress has revealed how 2-D, 3-D and 4-D powers – or Hall's (1997) larger environment – affect the encounter between citizens and welfare workers. The bureaucratic context and the procedures by which citizens (who claim to be ill despite lacking a biomedical diagnosis) are evaluated are important factors to bring to the analysis. The bureaucratic setup with medical consultants positioned within the municipalities alongside caseworkers seems to have strong effects on the perceived legitimacy of a citizen's illness (as identified by his or her own GP). Medical consultants only 'encounter' the patients' journals and are generally more sceptical towards citizens who experience vague illnesses, such as stress and depression. For this reason, the doctors (who meet the patients in the medical clinic) translate the symptoms into diagnoses, which they hope will have the intended effect – as seen from their perspective. In this process, the diagnosis 'stress-related depression' becomes central, as it is a clinical (and biomedically measurable) diagnosis compared with the label of stress. Even though both types of doctors evaluate the legitimacy of a citizen's condition based on his or her medical history, the nature and prevalence of the symptoms, the credibility of the described symptoms, the results of the evaluation and the consequent outcome of the case seem to be largely determined by the doctors' respective places of work (medical clinic versus municipality). The fact that citizens in Denmark can choose their own GP may also affect this process, as this choice (ensured by values from both the market and psychology) may bring unidentifiable biases to the case. If a citizen is unhappy with the work of (or collaboration with) the GP, then he or she may freely choose a different one, which, in turn, may render the medical statements of GPs more untrustworthy, as seen from the caseworker's perspective.

Another powerful context is the power of diagnoses. Some illnesses (such as stress) do not grant the citizen the 'patient label', and hence lead to lower (spousal-dependent) financial support, whereas other illnesses (such as depression) identify the citizen as legitimately ill and consequently provide him or her with the highest possible financial support, which – as mentioned – is given independently of spousal income. The two diagnoses have other powerful effects as well: to be depressed is a diagnosis that explicitly focuses on the individual's psyche and thereby draws attention away from the social aspect of the illness. In comparison, the stress diagnosis emphasises the social situation of citizens and points, for instance, to the work situation as the cause of illness. The solution to the problems of the depressed or the stressed are, in other words, vastly different, as the former entails the medical field and the work of doctors and points furthermore to the psychological state of the patient, whereas the latter entails the engagement of the social system and hence the bureaucratic field and emphasises the social problems of the client's life. On a societal level, there is currently an unprecedented increase in citizens whose symptoms are labelled as stress or depression, citizens who were previously identified as suffering from fibromyalgia and whiplash or other categories, which (also) direct attention to the (weak) psychological constitution of the citizens, but do so in a slightly different way than, for instance, work-related stress and psychological depression.

The presence and development of popular diagnoses point to a third powerful context, namely, that widely acknowledged and accepted diagnoses can affect the encounter and the evaluation of the citizens symptoms in favourable or unfavourable ways depending on the (sometimes conflicting) perspectives of citizens, doctors and caseworkers. Finally, the analysis has also exemplified and emphasised other powerful contexts, which affect the welfare work but are situated beyond the welfare encounter, such as the ICD10 test and the home pages of Psychiatry Foundation and the Association for Depression. These documents and web-based contexts all inform the ways in which the three participant groups may legitimately evaluate symptoms, which lack biomedical documentation.

Powerful discretion: evaluations of a client's worthiness and other contextual matters

This second case draws on a research project on the encounter between citizens and welfare workers in Danish rehabilitation centres (Mik-Meyer

2004).[2] The case is chosen because it shows how the micro-orientations in a client–staff encounter (also) reflect both bureaucratic principles and norms from psychology, such as empathy, compassion and putting the citizen first. This case emphasises those identifications which Holstein and Gubrium (2000: 154) refer to with the notions of 'the-self-according-to-this-agency' or 'personality-as-viewed-by-this-expert', as well as what one could term 'the-self-according-to-the-norms-of-psychology-and-bureaucracy'. This case shows how the identification of a citizen as someone suited for retirement is based on two factors: the evaluation of the client's motivation, willingness to cooperate and proactivity (worthiness) (the field of psychology), and legal and economic considerations (the field of bureaucracy). The organisation of the work in the studied rehabilitation centres ensures that the centre staff are in daily contact with the client. The staff are responsible for evaluating the psychosocial characteristics of the client and are – in this case – the ones who show empathy and compassion and support her wishes for early retirement, compared with the municipality caseworkers, who barely know the client and are generally quite sceptical towards her wishes. However, and compared with the centre staff, the municipality caseworker and her bureaucratic perceptions of the client are strongly influenced by the economic considerations of her workplace because Danish municipalities, in general, seek to limit the number of (expensive) early retirements.

The following analysis is especially inspired by the literature discussed in Chapter 7, as the organisation of rehabilitation work seems to stimulate a more empathic, compassionate, person-centred, informal and coaching relationship with the client. The goal of the centre staff is to help the clients voice their situation and thereby allow them to become participants in the decisions about their lives (Mik-Meyer 2004, 2007; Ferguson 2007). It is a soft kind of power because the goal of making clients voice their situation must be achieved in a particular way. In order to enter into a co-production relation with the welfare staff, the clients must appear as motivated, proactive and cooperative individuals in an effort to have their take on the situation heard and accepted by the centre staff. As this case will show, Mary is an example of one such client: she is powerful enough to make the centre staff adopt her perceptions of her situation (someone who should be granted early retirement) to such a degree that the centre staff even try to pass this view on to the municipality caseworker. The case thereby illustrates how the goal of centring the client as an expert on his or her own situation may actually result in a quite powerful citizen position, even though the description of a client – by the centre staff, as well as the client himself or herself – may emphasise weaknesses and other troubles, as is the case with Mary.

The analysis is primarily influenced by the dramaturgical approach of Goffman (1990b), which implies that an interaction is perceived as a performance created by the surroundings and the audience. Particularly central hereto are the concepts of front-stage and back-stage, as they emphasise how the negotiation of identities is, in fact, a strategic exercise that takes place in various norm-based contexts with differing degrees of formality. This focus on strategy is illustrated by the intentional actions and behaviours of the participants (as discussed in Chapter 4 with reference to Goffman's work on strategic interaction). The analysis draws on three sets of data: notes from four weekly staff meetings, audio recordings from an informal preliminary meeting in which the client is prepared for the meeting with the municipality caseworker and audio recordings from the formal meeting between the client, her husband, the centre staff and the municipality caseworker (as well as the present author).

The client (Mary) is a fifty-six-year-old woman who had worked as a childcare provider for thirty-seven years before she had to stop working due to a number of symptoms. The following quote is her own description of the time just before her sick leave took place and her subsequent enrolment in the rehabilitation centre:

Mary: Well, I almost couldn't walk. I am thankful to my colleagues who told the ones down at the office, 'It's just not working because Mary can't even walk the stroller with the children'. All of a sudden my body would just get stuck and hurt so badly, like you wouldn't believe. I couldn't move at all. I did realise that it just couldn't keep going on like this but, you know, then you think to yourself, 'Oh, it'll be fine. You can just take a few pain killers, then it'll be okay again. The summer holiday is almost here and...'. Well, I was hoping to be able to continue until my sixtieth birthday and then over, done. That had been my wish for many years. Also because of my husband's age – he turns sixty-eight this Saturday, you know? ...

Interviewer: How did the decision come about – that you were to be assigned to a rehabilitation centre?

Mary: That was my caseworker at the municipality.

Interviewer: What did she say?

Mary: Well, in the beginning she suggested that I could retract my medical leave and announce myself well again – and then go down to the job centre. Then I told her, 'But I'm not able to do that'. I absolutely knew that I wasn't. I couldn't. I mean, I couldn't even make it through a single work day. 'Oh, but, um, how did I feel about joining the labour market?' Well, I didn't feel very good about it because I had worked from home all those years. I had chosen it for myself, you know? It's what I feel the most comfortable with. What I feel the most secure and at ease with. Well, then she wanted to try to send me to a rehabilitation centre. 'Oh', I said, 'what's

that?' Because I had no idea what it was, you know? 'Well, it's this place
where they test your ability to work', she told me. 'Okay'.

In the rehabilitation centre, Mary kept expressing daily that she was in
pain, but also that she would love to work if only she were able to. As the
following excerpts from weekly staff meetings throughout a three-month
period illustrate, the limitations of Mary were especially emphasised by her
contact person, alongside the perception that Mary's will to work was high.

First staff meeting

Contact person: Mary suffers from ulcers; she is very worn and has a new
hip that causes her problems. She gets these bouts of dizziness.... She is
a sweet little lady who says that she would like to have a flex-job. She is a
very careful girl but would like to make coffee and tea and go grocery shopping for the day care centre. When I made this suggestion, her face lit up.
She would very much like to do that.

Second staff meeting

Contact person: She is a bit sad – you know. She is a little delicate flower. I
think that she is afraid that we'll push her too far. Because she has a new
hip that doesn't work very well and she has year-round allergies, changes
in the connective tissues in her lungs. I think that she'd like to get retirement benefits.

Social worker: We have to take a closer look at her. We can't say anything
about …

Contact person: [*Interrupts*] Yes, you're right. It's still too soon.

Third staff meeting

Contact person: She is not well at all. She looks terrible. Her face is completely
swollen. She would like to be given early retirement benefits.

Social worker: Are you at a point where you can make such a decision?

Contact person: No, we probably have to look at her a bit more.

Fourth staff meeting

Contact person: We have to set a meeting in place with the municipality. She
can't do very much. There is no work to be gotten from her. [*The parties
agree to set up a meeting in an effort to secure retirement benefits for Mary.*]

As these excerpts illustrate, the contact person was convinced about the
severity of Mary's physical condition at a very early stage but nevertheless
agreed with the social worker – and the norm of evaluating clients over a
three-month period – to work with Mary a bit longer before making a final
decision. After the routinised three months had passed, they all agreed that
this case was about early retirement benefits. The social worker was now

convinced that they were dealing with a cooperative client who had very few abilities to work, in other words, a legitimately ill person that should be shown empathy and compassion. He explained,

> Well, she wants to but she's a poor little one by now, you know, and she coughs and coughs and is just about unable to be here with us, you know? In my opinion, she's actually sick. She can't work, you know? If she in any way could, I have no doubt that she would want to.

Goffman's characterisation of back-stage performance seems particularly relevant to include in the analyses of the negotiations regarding the legitimacy of Mary's troubles. From a more general perspective, the activities of the rehabilitation centre can be regarded as taking place back-stage compared with the client's few meetings with the municipality caseworker (front-stage). Many of the activities in the rehabilitation centre have in common that they must appear as quite informal (for instance, morning gatherings, trips outside the facilities, participation in hobby-like activities in various workshops and informal group conversations about private matters), the intention being that the client will 'let go of her mask' so that the centre staff can gain a more honest and credible impression of the client's situation and consequently his or her options.

This impression of a client shall then later on – approximately after three months, as in the case of Mary – be delivered to the client's municipality caseworker through a series of formalised meetings. The participation of the client in the activities provided by the rehabilitation centre and the staff's subsequent evaluation should ideally be based only on the abilities of the particular client, whereas the municipality caseworker's assessment to a much greater degree is based on the possibilities given by both legislation and the local political and economic conditions. It is typically the task of the social workers of the rehabilitation centres to (try to) find common ground between these two very different positions of interest and knowledge. In this particular case, the social worker decides to evaluate Mary in accordance with the evaluations of the contact person and Mary herself, an evaluation that greatly contrasts the municipality caseworker's evaluation of her, as the analysis will show.

In those cases where opinions differ regarding the evaluation of a client's situation, the social workers of the rehabilitation centres will automatically be positioned as very central staff members as they coordinate the work between these two organisations (municipality and rehabilitation centre). In the example of Mary, the staff agrees on a description of her which reflects her own self descriptions. The (powerful) process of categorisation is in this case positive and productive for the client and can be regarded as reflecting the agency and habitus of Mary, who apparently has learned to focus on problems in a legitimate way in an effort to be evaluated as suited for retirement. However, the ambiguous position of the social workers of the rehabilitation centre – due to the fact that they act in a back-stage environment (such as the informal activities in the centre) while doing front-stage work (such as the formal, procedural-oriented activities through their contact with the municipality) – means that even though they must strive to create an informal and honest relationship with the client, they must still adhere to the principles and routines of the municipality (Maynard-Moody and Musheno 2003; Lipsky 2010). This ambiguous position may partly explain the existence of the routinised (but informal) meeting with the client prior to the joint meeting with the client's municipality caseworker. During this 'pre-meeting', the social worker will have the opportunity to head off any surprised reactions the client may be presenting during the formal meeting or – as in the case of Mary – to calm the client prior to the formal meeting.

Another important reason for this informal meeting is that it provides an opportunity to adjust the presentation of the client's situation. During this meeting, the client is informed about how the centre staff evaluates her situation and is given the opportunity to object to this evaluation. However, because the meeting is held just prior to the formal meeting with the municipality caseworker, there is very little room for discussing or addressing any major disagreements among the staff or between staff and client.

The routinised informal meeting between client, contact person and social worker

Mary and her contact person are having a conversation before the social worker arrives. The contact person provides Mary with several calming phrases. She says, for instance, 'We don't disagree at all about what should happen to you, so you can just relax'. Mary admits to being quite nervous about the coming meeting, as there is 'a lot at stake for me', as she puts it. After a few minutes, the social worker arrives and says with a smile that there is absolutely nothing to be nervous about. 'Your case is easy, Mary', he tells her. The meeting begins.

Social worker: [*Looks in Mary's journal*] You have seen a medical specialist?

Mary: Yes, I'll receive some answers soon.

Social worker: Any changes throughout the past two weeks?

Mary: No.

Social worker: Ability to work?

Mary: Minimal.

Social worker: One hour?

Mary: At most.

Social worker: We have to assume that this won't change in time. Our recommendation is therefore that you finalise your stay here at the centre. The conclusion is that your ability to work is not useful for the labour market. In two or three weeks' time, we will send the final report to the municipality. We won't write the word *retirement* but will phrase it differently. In regards to the upcoming meeting [with the caseworker from the municipality], we usually do it so it is the person whom the case is about, who tells about his or her situation.

Mary: [*Sounding a bit nervous*]: So, me?

Social worker: Yes, but not in any fancy words. You just talk about how you feel. Where are you from again?

Mary: X municipality.

Social worker: That's a very good municipality to have a retirement case in. They'll get it done quickly [*laughs*]. You are a lucky one, you know that? [*In a more serious tone of voice*] I can't imagine that they'll need anything else. The physiotherapist will in addition make a statement.

Mary: But I haven't been visiting the physiotherapist [at the centre].

Social worker: No, but she will write that you have been unable to. In this case, our doctor will also write a statement about you. We will inform him and then he usually writes a conclusion that supports our assessment. We will explain to him your situation and then we have some statements from doctors. [*In a declaring and final tone of voice*] So that's a good thing.

Mary: So I can just take the day off on Friday?

Social worker: Yes, then the retirement case will be in the works.

Mary: I assume I will get the least amount of benefits since my husband has a job?

Social worker: No, the benefits are given according to your ability to work. So probably mid-level benefits since your ability to work is so little. And you have actually gotten worse since you came here. [*The meeting comes to an end with a bit of casual conversation.*]

It is during this meeting that the subsequent play is planned, rehearsed and familiarised. The meeting begins with a brief questioning of Mary in order to conclude that there is no discernible 'ability to work'. Note how Mary is made aware of several aspects, which – undoubtedly – would have been quite problematic to discuss in the presence of her municipality caseworker, such as how she lives in a 'good' municipality in regards to receiving early retirement benefits and that the centre doctor and physiotherapist will each write an assessment that supports the view of the contact person and social worker (even though Mary has seen neither the doctor nor the physiotherapist). This pre-meeting illustrates the negotiation of the legitimacy of Mary's symptoms as a process in which the staff collaborates strategically with Mary in an effort to ensure a certain (and for Mary, desirable) outcome.

The routinised formal meeting with centre staff, Mary, her husband and the municipality caseworker

As the analysis of the meeting reveals, the centre staff does not regard Mary's case as particularly difficult. The many statements from doctors written prior to her stay at the centre and a few additional (and more recent) expert statements, alongside the observations of her gradually declining condition, appear – in their eyes – to be sufficient for them to guarantee that she will be granted her desired status within a short amount of time. Even though the centre staff agrees in their description of Mary's situation, it will take more work, as well as a certain contextual competence in the dialogue with the municipal caseworker, to get the caseworker to support their opinion of Mary's situation. The presentation of Mary's physical state has to be compared with the municipality-sanctioned description of what it takes to be qualified for retirement in her municipality. The meeting begins with informal conversation that turns into a question to Mary about her everyday life at the centre.

> Mary: I arrive in the morning and then I just get worse and worse throughout the day. There is something here that doesn't agree with me.
>
> Municipal caseworker: Allergies?
>
> Mary: Yes, I don't know.
>
> Municipal caseworker: Is it a stress factor or is there something you are allergic to?
>
> Mary: I don't feel stressed. I am very happy to be here.
>
> Municipal caseworker: [*Asserting*] So it has occurred before.
>
> Social worker: Mary, can you tell us a bit about your work and rhythm?
>
> Mary: I am able to work at most ten minutes at a time. Often, I have to leave earlier than that. I simply can't be here.
>
> Social worker: Are there any more examinations you need to have?
>
> Mary: No.
>
> Contact person: [*Approaching Mary*] You have been very stable and very willing. It is usually me who has to make you stop.
>
> Municipal caseworker: Is there anything else that affects you?
>
> Mary: Everything hurts. When I cough, my entire body hurts.
>
> Municipal caseworker: So it's the coughing?
>
> Mary: No, it is also my leg and my hip, and I'm not even able to ride my bike.
>
> Municipal caseworker: What do the doctors say?
>
> Mary: Nothing. They say that it looks fine. I am so sick of doctors.

Social worker: We have also talked a bit about her appetite with our doctor because Mary has ulcers as well.

Mary: Yes, I take medicine against ulcers.

Contact person: You have lost weight while you've been here.

Municipal caseworker: Do you currently have an ulcer, Mary?

Mary: It was still open in 1996. A year ago, I was given four bags of blood, and it stings and burns still every now and again, and it has gotten worse from me being here.

Contact person: You also have a fever.

Mary: Last time the doctors told me that if the fever didn't go away, then they would have to admit me. But they haven't been able to figure it out.

Municipal caseworker: So they haven't been able to detect it?

Mary: No. [*Mary begins to state a series of numbers regarding her medical condition. She talks quickly and for a long time.*]

Social worker: There have been times where you've had problems with your liver enzymes.

Mary: Yes. [*Mary talks again and for a long time about all her problems prior to the surgery where she received a new hip.*]

Municipal caseworker: Yes, that was your leg. Because you are in the process of being examined, we have to wait for the results.

Social worker: Yes, but there is nothing more for us to do here. [*In an assertive tone of voice*] There is no attainable change, and there is no ability to work, which would make an internship a possibility.

Municipal caseworker: Let's make a small thought experiment, imaging if we could find a workplace where you could be without getting sick. It would be a good thing if we could figure out what it is that doesn't agree with you. It would be a really good thing, if we could figure that one out.

Contact person: No, that would have to be a workplace without people. [*Approaching Mary*] That day with the folders, that wasn't good for you at all. And that day in our workshop with the fabrics, that didn't work for you either.

Mary: No, it's because I am allergic to birch and therefore there are many things I can't be around. I have taken up to four tablets a day [*referring to allergy medicine*], and you are only supposed to take two – but it's because it's so lovely to be here. People are so nice, so I've taken too many.

Municipal caseworker: If the medical documentation states that it is a chronic condition, then not much improvement can be made. That settles it then.

Social worker: Have you been evaluated by the allergy clinic?

Mary: Yes, a few years ago. But when they were to do more tests, then the thing with my hip happened and they couldn't do anything because my allergies are year-round.

Municipal caseworker: But your condition has worsened and that's why we have to look at what the medical documentation tells us. You experience pains in your legs, but those are chronic and you are aware of them.

Mary: Yes, it hurts all the time.

Municipal caseworker: Then you have ulcers, but not as much anymore. Then there is the allergy, which is the one factor that has actually gotten worse.

Contact person: But that became a lot worse after you had been to relaxation treatment.

Municipal caseworker: There are three days until Easter [pause]. I guess that your own doctor has to make an overall evaluation of all these things. I can't see any other options than that we'll have to wait for that evaluation.

Social worker: So will she have to stay here until it arrives?

Municipal caseworker: Yes, that would be good.

Social worker: Pointless. We can revisit this idea if it turns out that there are possibilities for treatment.

Municipal caseworker: So, should we end the meeting here?

Social worker: Yes, I think so. [Approaching Mary] In our experience, you do everything you can. And there is no resistance against work ability tests because if there were, it would be a quite different story.

Municipal caseworker: When did you stop working with the children?

Mary: Two years ago. [She begins to talk about her allergies again for a long time while coughing.]

Municipal caseworker: I can't see any options other than that we have to make sure that there are absolutely no possibilities for treatment.

Mary's husband: But her hip is also a problem.

Municipal caseworker: Yes, but it is possible to take that into consideration. As I see it, it is the allergies, which take up all her energy.

Mary's husband: She also has arthritis in her fingers.

Municipal caseworker: Pardon?

Mary's husband: She has severe arthritis in her fingers.

Municipal caseworker: Yes, but light office work could possibly be ...

Contact person: [Interrupts] So she can sit and cough into the telephone ...

Social worker: [Interrupts in an annoyed tone of voice] That's what needs to be tested.

Municipal caseworker: Yes, but take ulcers, for instance, many people work with ulcers. So if you consider these singular things, they don't affect your ability to work. But the allergy does.

[The contact person and Mary start talking about all the things Mary is allergic to, for instance, the flower in the office, and that she can't go grocery shopping because *of the many different types of food. Mary says that it is only in her own home that she isn't bothered as much or doesn't cough as much.*]

Mary: Yes, but I guess that we have to wait until we have some test results.

Municipal caseworker: It is a bit odd that you only cough here. That when in the comfort of your own home, then you don't cough. That's strange.

Mary: But it doesn't go away at home. I cough at home too.

Municipal caseworker: But you just said that it lessened whenever you are home.

Mary: That is true. But I cough very extremely for about an hour every morning and so much that I throw up. And that's every morning.

The meeting ends and the social worker accompanies the municipal caseworker to the door. The contact person assures Mary that the meeting went as it should, and when the social worker returns he says, 'Congratulations. That turned out just like we wanted it to'. Mary asks her husband to wait for her while she fetches her things in the workshop. On her way to the workshop, Mary explains how she thought the meeting went:

Oh, I just got so annoyed with my husband for saying that thing about my hip. I had told him not to interfere. He shouldn't have said anything about the hip because that argument doesn't count. It is the thing with my allergies. That was supposed to be my life raft and keep me from continuing in the system.

As the excerpts show, both the centre staff and Mary tried to convince the municipality caseworker to begin procedures for early retirement benefits. This goal explains the somewhat one-sided discussions during the meeting, as well as the problem-focused descriptions of Mary. In the words of Goffman, the roles have been cast and the play has been arranged (during previous staff meetings and the pre-meeting with Mary). The role available to the municipal caseworker was the one of a saviour who sets the work in motion that will lead to Mary's early retirement. However, the municipality caseworker did not seem willing to accept the role of the saviour at first, as the discussion of Mary's symptoms illustrates. She decided instead to play the part of a critical investigator whose aim was to challenge the somewhat exaggerated illness descriptions presented by the centre staff, Mary's husband and Mary herself. As it turns out, the municipal caseworker was also cast in another play: a play that seeks to minimise the number of (expensive) early retirement applications in her municipality. These two conflicting definitions of the situation (Goffman 1990b) clash throughout the meeting as the municipality caseworker continuously tries to discredit Mary's statements and the centre staff's evaluation of her.

The municipality caseworker's very technical approach to evaluating the physical situation of Mary – in which she assesses each ailment or symptom on its own and then tries to determine whether it has occurred before – provides information about the municipal procedures of determining a client's eligibility for early retirement benefits; it reflects, in other words, the formal front-stage procedures and principles. The approach of the municipality caseworker is moreover in direct conflict with the expertise of the centre staff (and especially that of the contact person), which revolves around sensing the overall situation of a client (based on back-stage activities) and coaching her in the best possible way. To be confronted with the formal and quite technical dissection of Mary's situation therefore provokes the contact person: the presence of an ulcer is in itself insufficient to qualify for early retirement, as are a new hip that gets stuck from time to time, pains in the legs, arthritis in the fingers, changes in the connective tissues in the lungs, problems with liver enzymes, too small an appetite and weight loss – and a combination of all of these symptoms, for that matter. However, allergy is a sufficient condition. The municipality caseworker perceives the allergy as the one factor that actually matters, which is probably due to the fact that it is the only one of Mary's many ailments that has yet to be medically assessed (or thoroughly at least) and is the only ailment that can prevent her from working – regardless of the situation – as allergies may occur anytime and anywhere. Allergy is the one ailment of Mary's which is still medically unproven and which therefore (in principle at least) may live up to the bureaucratic demand for biomedical documentation of symptoms.

Mary's husband fails to grasp this special status of his wife's allergies and accidentally annoys her when mentioning her problems with her hip and the arthritis in her fingers, especially because the allergies – according to Mary herself – may be her life raft and the one factor that can prevent her from staying in the system, as she explains after the meeting. Because the previous occurrence of allergy symptoms is apparently quite difficult to assess – perhaps because this illness is a recent addition to the client's medical history and is less well known and less stable than her other ailments – these particular symptoms are given a special status. During the meeting, the agency of Mary is also evaluated, that is, her ability throughout the meeting to evaluate the different illnesses and whether they will help her gain the status of early retirement recipient. She furthermore seems aware of key norms of the market and psychological contexts, namely, that she ought to be a responsive, cooperative, proactive and willing-to-work kind of person, who would be self-supporting if only she could.

However, Mary's husband does not seem to have understood that they must focus on Mary's allergy (and not her inability to walk or her arthritis) when trying to solve her problem situation. He thus demonstrates a lack of knowledge of bureaucratic processes and evaluations of symptoms. It is furthermore possible that lay perceptions of allergies as, for instance, expressions of hypochondria or attention seeking cause him to perceive the more tangible physical ailments, such as inability to walk or arthritis, as more valid. However, neither inability to walk nor arthritis is on the municipal list of ailments which qualify for early retirement. To talk about these troubles therefore falls under Goffman's (1967: 8) concept of wrong face, as they will not activate the preferred 'eligible for early retirement' category.

Notice, moreover, how Mary's presentation of herself (Goffman 1967) changes as the situational definition of the municipality caseworker – who emphasises the relevant procedures – becomes more and more dominant in the encounter. The self-presentations of the interacting parties (except for Mary's husband) may be viewed as an altogether successful enterprise, because they bring together their situational definitions with the winning definition of the municipality caseworker and her focus on allergies. Throughout the meeting, Mary learns to emphasise her allergic reactions and to describe in great detail how they limit her in everyday life. She becomes more and more 'in face' (Goffman 1967). The same thing happens with the social worker and the contact person of the rehabilitation centre; however, it takes them a bit longer to adjust to the winning definition of the situation. The situational definition of the municipality caseworker – which reflects the procedures of early retirement in Mary's residential municipality – can thus be regarded as governing the progression of the meeting. Even though it requires a bit of work for both the centre staff and Mary to adjust their presentations of her in a way which aligns with the play of the municipality caseworker, the meeting pretty much concludes as wished. The casting of Mary by the rehabilitation centre as someone who should be shown empathy, is physically worn, only has a few employable years left before qualifying for (normal) retirement and shows a great amount of will and cooperation, and therefore – from a holistic approach that values the willingness of citizens to better their situations – should qualify for early retirement, is thus transformed (and quite surprisingly so, from their perspective) into a discussion about allergic reactions.

Even though the municipality caseworker does not focus explicitly on the will of Mary – for instance, her expressions of will in the rehabilitation centre – one should not deny the beneficial effects of the centre staff's continuous referral to Mary as showing cooperation, motivation and will (showcasing a worthy client [Maynard-Moody and Musheno 2000: 93–94]). It is likely that the staff's emphasis on her extraordinary will to work (if only she could) and her willingness to cooperate is the main reason for why the municipality caseworker in the end agrees that Mary will not have to stay in the rehabilitation centre while they await further evaluation from her doctor (as initially suggested by her). It is furthermore likely that it is the willingness and cooperation of Mary that causes the contact person to refer to the idea of Mary remaining at the centre as 'pointless'. The extraordinary willingness and motivation of Mary, highly praised characteristics in Denmark (and in Western societies in general), thus seem to be essential factors in deciding that she has no 'ability to work' and that the situation will not 'change in time', as the social worker puts it. The assumption that Mary embodies these valued norms – that she does everything she can and would love to work if she were able to – illustrates the moral work of the staff and means that in the end (and in a more general sense), the centre staff's definition of the situation becomes the winning one.

Concluding comments

When critically examining both negative and positive client identifications, such as 'deadlocked clients' or 'flexible and motivated clients' (as in the case with Mary), it is of paramount importance to examine how these identifications are based on, for instance, principles of how to evaluate the resources of clients and norms of ideal client behaviour. In this second case of rehabilitation, the organisation of the welfare work (e.g., formality versus informality), combined with the municipality's procedures for early retirement qualification, had a great impact on the evaluation of the client's resources. Client identifications may thus first and foremost provide information about the organisational context in which they are produced, rather than the individuals they appear to describe. Furthermore, these descriptions are not always negative for the client, as much research seems to indicate; these descriptions can actually be constructive and of benefit to the process of evaluating the resources of a client, as shown in the case of Mary.

However, these descriptions take place in a context of power-over, which defines what is perceived as legitimate and relevant and thus structures the 2-D rules of the encounter. By complying with this power, the relationship between Mary and the contact person generates a power-with in the team, which results in power-to for Mary (she is empowered to retire). However, and in contrast, her husband – although having the best of intentions – behaves inappropriately in this context. His behaviour may stem from a social incompetence, as defined by the bureaucratic context and its capitals, because he (unlike Mary) has not been shaped by the 3-D or 4-D power. Neither has he learned to recognise the valid grounds of this context (3-D power), nor does he possess the right dispositions (4-D). In contrast, Mary is exemplary from the perspectives of both 3-D (she knows what is relevant) and 4-D (she has the right social disposition, as manifested by her apparent willingness to work).

In her case, the – after some negotiation – joint description of Mary as a willing and motivated person who unfortunately suffered from allergies meant that all parties of the encounter could (finally) work together towards securing an early retirement for her. This label of 'suitable for pension' was of great importance for Mary, as it meant that her legal and economic situation would no longer be as uncertain as was the case when she initially was referred to the rehabilitation centre. In other words, to be lacking a category affiliation is very problematic for clients, as the legal right to economic compensation is based on category affiliation. To be labelled according to her troubles (e.g., arthritis in the fingers, pains in the legs and changes in the connective tissues in the lungs) did not secure the much wanted status of 'qualified for early retirement'; however, the (positive) labelling of Mary as cooperative and motivated, in combination with her problems with allergies, did secure her placement in the category 'qualified for early retirement' (pending further evaluations). Category affiliation is, in other words, not only necessary for the rehabilitation centres who determine the nature and scope of the problems of clients and whose goal is to translate the troubles of clients into the social categories of the welfare state (Järvinen and Mik-Meyer 2003, 2012; Gubrium and Järvinen 2014a). It is also absolutely essential for the clients, who – as in the case of Mary – are then given certainty regarding their future income bases and possible activities.

It is thus very problematic to not belong to a category while being dependent on the social system. Many clients of the welfare state have extensive work experience and have become accustomed to a life with a stable financial income. When they lose their jobs – due to, for instance, physical or mental occupational injuries or cutbacks in their work organisations – and are referred to the social system for welfare benefits and support, the categorisation process then begins. It would be wrong to assume that clients such as Mary are unaware of how their actions and attitudes affect the evaluation and decisions regarding their legal and financial situations in the welfare field, that is, to assume that clients per definition are individuals who do not work strategically to better their situation. For this reason, it is important to study welfare encounters with emphasis on the norms and rationales of the fields in question, which regulate the encounter (in this case, motivation, willingness to cooperate, rules and procedures of the municipality, etc.), as well as the agency of both clients and welfare workers as both parties affect the progression of the interaction. Clients who, for instance, demonstrate plenty of will but little ability to work will most likely be regarded by staff as legitimately ill (even in cases where the medical documentation is missing). Such clients will, in other words, carefully choose how to present themselves in the encounter with welfare workers in an effort to achieve their desired outcomes.

The goal of the analysis of this second case was to demonstrate the importance of applying a relational approach to welfare encounters, as doing so brings the habitus and the agency of the client to the forefront. This goal is especially important because much research tends to overlook the fact that even clients who seem weak at first glance (such as Mary) can actually be powerful participants in welfare encounters, if one examines whose definition of the situation prevails or who holds the dominant capital of the investigated field. The goal of the analysis was furthermore to showcase how norms from psychology – strategies of personalisation and co-production; coaching relationships with clients; empathic, compassionate and informal ways of contact between clients and staff; and so forth – greatly impact the welfare encounter, even when concealed by the soft and gentle approach of welfare workers. It is, after all, not all clients who will succeed in transferring their view of their (problem) situation onto the welfare workers. It requires, in other words, a certain level of skill to come across as exactly as weak and troubled (as in the case with Mary) so that the welfare workers will perceive the problems told by clients as credible and legitimate. This focus on skills, the ability to affect the welfare encounter in a particular way, is also applicable to resourceful clients who, for instance, want the welfare staff to work hard(er) to find them employment: they too must work to appear exactly as resourceful as defined by the welfare context so the welfare workers will perceive them as legitimate actors and thus regard their wishes as appropriate.

Notes

1. This case draws on publications from my research on MUS, especially Chapter 6 in Mik-Meyer and Johansen (2009).
2. This case draws on publications from my research on rehabilitation practices, especially Chapter 5 in Mik-Meyer (2004).

9

Conclusion

Within the field of social sciences, it is widely recognised that current welfare states operate by a rationale of steering their citizens, which is vastly different from the approach of welfare states in the 1970s and 1980s. The shift of the 1990s towards a so-called governance approach to the citizens has gradually and over time increased in strength and has resulted in a particular framing of the encounter between welfare workers and citizens. A governance approach to the citizen has, among other goals, to do with prioritising the involvement of citizens and local communities in solving social problems (Brugnoli and Colombo 2012: xi). It is an approach that not only aims at solving practical issues; it is moreover designed to resolve the moral problems of presumably passive citizens and communities. Consequently, a governance approach assigns the responsibility for resolving the (problematic) situations of citizens to the citizens themselves, and in doing so creates new tasks for welfare workers, who are now supposed to service and coach the imaginably active and responsible citizens.

This strengthened focus on the actions of the individual citizen is described by terms such as co-production, co-responsibilisation, empowerment, user participation and user involvement (Newman and Tonkens 2011a; Evers and Guillemard 2013). Even though there may be a real (political) wish to involve citizens in how to define, handle and solve their problems, a number of studies have nevertheless shown that their involvement is very much controlled by the welfare workers, the legal framework and the principles of the bureaucracy and market (Rose 2000; Clarke 2005; Clarke et al. 2007; Cowden and Singh 2007).

The focus of this book has been on how welfare workers and citizens translate and implement the principles of the bureaucracy, the values of the market and the norms from psychology in everyday welfare work, that is, how rule-abiding conduct, legal certainty and so forth (bureaucracy); ideals of servicing the citizens and giving them the freedom of choice (market);

and showing empathy and engaging in co-productive relations (psychology) affect the encounter between welfare workers and citizens.

A central focus of this book is how the governance approach to citizens has altered the perceptions and encounters of citizens and welfare workers and, in particular, in relation to the idea of empowered, active and responsible citizens. In an effort to analyse these new positions of citizens and welfare workers, it turned out to be most fruitful to use a power perspective that could combine 2-D, 3-D and 4-D power approaches, an approach that could bring the power-over and power-to together in an analysis (Haugaard 2012). Consequently, the main task has not been to merely investigate how hard power (such as 2-D legislative powers) affects the welfare work. Instead, a softer kind of power and its effects on the welfare encounter have been examined as well, one that draws on both the particular norms of the welfare workers and the expectations of 'appropriate' behaviour of citizens (3-D and 4-D powers). Because 3-D and 4-D powers are not easily recognised by the encountering parties, the concept of soft power (and the linguistic qualities of this concept) illustrates that the power at play is indeed both soft (i.e., gentle and indulgent) and powerful, as it – despite its softer nature – both frames and governs the welfare encounter.

The analysis of the book has found three levels of power at play in these encounters. At a 2-D level, we have a bureaucratic context which merits certain rules and procedures. At a 3-D level, we have the interpretive horizon of the social actors who perceive a taken-for-granted reality or natural order of things. At a 4-D level, we have social subjects whose actions reflect the rules of the bureaucracy, as well as the values of the market and norms from psychology. For instance, the allergy case of Chapter 8 showed that the municipality caseworker took a 3-D perspective when she took it for granted that allergies were valid while a painful hip was not (according to 2-D powers of the municipal bureaucratic procedures). This evaluation turned out to be in stark contrast to the perceptions of Mary's husband, who failed to internalise this 3-D sense-making, as he had not been subjected to the same socialisation as the rehabilitation centre staff (by the municipality) or Mary (by the rehabilitation centre). At a 4-D level, Mary thus became a particular kind of subject, someone who was determined and willing to work, but unable to do so for more than a limited period of time. She performed, in other words, the role of the active and responsible individual, a 4-D social subject.

In order to investigate how (legitimate) welfare work is conducted, one needs, in other words, to apply a concept of power that unites the 2-D, 3-D and 4-D approaches. This combination ensures an analysis that can show how the dominant rules and principles of the bureaucracy and the central norms of today's society (to be responsible, independent, proactive, etc.) produce legitimate encounters and 'good citizens' (Pykett *et al.* 2010). The legitimacy of the encounter rests on whether the actions of citizens can be viewed as liberated from the pacifying welfare state, whether citizens are capable of making choices and voicing their situation and whether they show (adequate levels of) responsibility in their decision-making. However, an important question raised by Clarke and colleagues (2005: 448–454) is whether this particular norm-based approach to citizens actually leads to the abandonment of citizens who lack these personal resources and who – for this very reason – are no longer worthy of the help of the welfare state.

Thus, the present governance approach infused by norms and assumptions of active, responsible individuals also reveals its own disadvantages, as these norms wrongly assume that all citizens are capable of taking on the demanding position of the active, empowered and responsible welfare subject. Failing to do so – as many citizens in fact do – they are then left to their own devices. In addition, when citizens demonstrate their abilities of making choices and voicing their situation, the welfare encounter may still be challenging, as this new citizen position may threaten the traditional expert position of the welfare staff (especially in situations in which the encountering parties disagree on how to perceive and resolve the problem situation at hand). Furthermore, this threatening of the expertise of the welfare staff may not be caused solely by the reframing of citizens as experts in their own lives: the expertise of welfare workers may furthermore be threatened by additional bureaucracy-induced principles and rules of how to conduct good welfare work.

The professionalism of welfare workers

This ambiguity of the roles of staff in their encounter with citizens has led Evetts (2009a, 2009b) to suggest the distinction between two ideal typical contexts of professionalism today: organisational professionalism (governed by organisational norms) and occupational professionalism (governed by professional norms). Her argument is that the professionalism of staff is currently (perhaps even mostly) influenced by organisational norms, that is, principles and rules of the bureaucracy in combination with performance measurement strategies of the market (and a goal of empathic and compassionate relationships with the individual inspired by the field of psychology). According to Evetts, the context of welfare work is saturated with (new) norms which completely change the encounter between welfare workers and citizens (Evetts 2011: 412, 416).

The point is that current welfare staff are perhaps not predominantly steered by professional norms and ethics, combined with the welfare workers' capabilities to apply bureaucratically based discretion in their work, as is found in many Lipsky-inspired studies. Present-day welfare encounters may instead be steered by the (political) goals of the organisation (such as achievement targets and performance indicators) or by the aim of approaching citizens as individuals who are capable of making choices and acting in responsible ways. This development indicates that the best way of examining welfare encounters today is by investigating how the principles and norms from the market and psychology also affect the encounter, principles and norms which differ greatly from those of the bureaucracy.

In following this line of thought, welfare workers are perhaps not making judgements based on a so-called pure professionalism, which centres around disciplinary knowledge, skills, experience, jurisdictional control, knowledge transfer and codes of conduct, as discussed at length in the sociology of professions. The judgements of welfare workers may instead stem from so-called situated and hybridised forms of professionalism, which emphasise a reflexive form of control, the ability to form 'meaningful connections' between citizens and welfare workers (Noordegraaf 2007: 780). The notion of meaningful connections is obviously a contextual construct, as it will vary from context to context and in accordance with the dominant ideals of how to define the problems of citizens in meaningful ways.

In contrast to the commonly accepted knowledge within the sociology of professions, organisational and societal norms perhaps do not relate primarily 'to the power of the professionals' knowledge systems' (Abbott 1988: 30), as the current contexts of these interactions are much more complex and contested. If, for instance, a welfare encounter is dominated by a rational-legal way of thinking (as in the bureaucracy), then powerful individuals will be those who succeed in activating and employing resources, which fit with a rational-legal way of legitimising actions and behaviours. If the welfare encounter, on the other hand, is dominated by a market rationale, then powerful individuals will be those who succeed in employing resources which fit with a market-oriented way of rationalising.

Essentially, as argued by Bourdieu, powerful participants are those who have learned the rules of a specific field in order to gain the necessary capital to exercise power. As all actors are situated within a nexus of fields (e.g., the fields of bureaucracy and psychology), they must become skilled at drawing on various fields simultaneously, thus navigating a complex and contested terrain. In learning the rules of multiple games, citizens and welfare staff become shaped with certain dispositions which constitute a subtle form of

4-D power. As these social actors are subjected to both field specific power and empowered agents, this process is both top-down and bottom-up, an amalgam of power-over, power-with and power-to (Haugaard 2012).

All chapters have consequently refrained from employing essentialising representations of both organisations and individuals, as doing so wrongly assumes agency as (merely) the property of individual subjects or organisations (2-D power). Welfare encounters should also be viewed as the outcomes of specific dominant ideas about what it takes to be regarded as 'good' or 'bad' citizens today (3-D power). The agency of both citizens and welfare workers has, in other words, to do with interconnectedness, interaction and intersubjectivity (4-D power). Agency is, as such, a relational and dynamic concept that illustrates a fundamental principle of human interaction. Thus, a person's self cannot be separated from the selves of those with whom he or she interacts, which is why agency (with reference to scholars such as Goffman) must be regarded as 'profoundly enmeshed with shared expectations and accomplished in everyday life through interaction' (Wright 2012: 318). The agency of both welfare workers and citizens is negotiated in the contexts of policymaking, dominant perceptions of how to perceive and solve the problem at hand, existing rules and procedures and so forth. This means that the actions of both welfare workers and citizens cannot be regarded Instead: as, for instance, solely those of economic-rational actors who each operate with their 'own' interests in mind, as if these interests were isolated entities unaffected by the policy context, the other encountering parties or similar important factors (Hunter 2003: 332).

Institutional selves and the larger environment

For this reason, the book has furthermore introduced the reader to symbolic interactionism, because this tradition within sociology makes it possible to examine how welfare workers and citizens co-produce dominant powerful norms in the welfare encounter. At the heart of symbolic interactionism are the practices and actions between people, as well as the question of how these can be perceived as the effects of different ideas and theories within organisations and societies. Citizens' and welfare workers' identifications and perceptions (of both themselves and each other) are within an interactionist tradition regarded as the results of social processes and are therefore presumed to be created and recreated in and by social interactions. A key focus within this tradition is thus how interacting individuals interpret the particular situations of which they are part, as this research tradition regards interpretations as having real consequences for the actors, their interactions, their perceptions of others and their self-identifications (Mik-Meyer and Villadsen 2014).

In order for an interaction to be rid of conflict, it is therefore essential that the participants agree about what kind of situation they engage in. For instance, does a situation revolve around getting a job, talking about a personal problem or a third matter? Should the citizen expect service, legal advice or coaching from the welfare worker, and conversely, should the welfare worker expect to encounter a citizen who wants to be serviced, receive legal advice or be coached? As the many examples of the book have shown, it is easy to imagine scenarios where the encountering parties do not agree on how to define the situation of which they are part, which, in turn, means that they will try to make their take on the situation the winning definition or – if this is impossible – accept and adjust to the role put forth by the other participant and his or her (winning) definition.

The concept of institutional selves (e.g., Gubrium and Holstein 2001) illustrates that different situations, such as welfare encounters, lead to different institutional identifications. Therefore, when participants are expected to act in a certain way (and thus to express specific institutional selves), then the aim of research inspired by symbolic interactionism is to examine how the observed institutional selves relate to the social context in which their actions take place and are meaningful. The aim of doing so is to examine how social selves relate to their context rather than achieve a more nuanced, deeper or better understanding of the particular individual and his or her social problems as detached from the specific organisational context.

However, the particular institutional perceptions of citizens and welfare workers not only reflect a local organisational reality, they also reflect societal trends of how to conduct professional welfare work (as illustrated in policy reports, societal debates, etc.). Institutional perceptions are affected by other, more general structural features than the gender, race and social class of the encountering parties; the asymmetry between welfare workers and citizens; and so on. They are also affected by certain norm-systems which render specific roles – such as facilitators, coaches and experts – obvious. These expectations of individuals (both welfare workers and citizens) thus produce particular behavioural possibilities and limitations. Institutional selves is therefore a concept that not only applies to work conducted within physical organisations or workplaces but also relates to 'a larger environment' (Hall 1997). This larger environment – the different norm-systems and rationales – means that citizens may not be the only ones who are subjected to, for instance, a so-called clientisation process, which indicates a process of dependency (Gubrium and Järvinen 2014a). Welfare workers may similarly find themselves in a dependency relation formed by powerful policies, which establish certain norms and expectations of how to properly conduct work in today's welfare organisations.

For this reason, Hall's (1997) suggested meta-power approach (a combi-nation of 2-D, 3-D and 4-D power analyses) is important, as this approach makes it possible to explore how the social organisation of a situation relates to the principles and norms beyond it. The goal of such meso-domain anal-yses is to investigate how the interactions of individuals can be regarded as the products of the actions and behaviours of the participants, as well as the structures and histories of the investigated fields. Hall (1997) focuses in particular on policy agents and how the actions of this group of people are affected by the awareness that their work impacts the work (lives) of welfare workers and citizens. In other words, welfare workers – the front-line staff – are affected not only by specific policy agendas but also by the fact that their actions and decisions can have many important consequences for the citizens whom they encounter. Furthermore, the actions of citizens reflect both the (policy) agenda of the particular encounter and their own interpretations of how their actions may either strengthen or weaken the possibility of achieving what they want from the welfare encounter. Even if the effects of the larger environment are unobservable when analysing a single welfare encounter, the larger environment will become visible when investigating several encounters, and even more so when relating the find-ings of such investigations to other sociological work, which explores and studies similar phenomena.

The three contexts

The principles of the bureaucracy are an important context for the encounter between welfare workers and citizens, as citizen–staff encoun-ters per definition are regulated by legislation and local principles related to the bureaucracy. Therefore, if one assumes that the commitment to rule-abiding conduct, legal certainty and so on does not govern these interac-tions, then one is very much mistaken, as convincingly shown in the classic work of Lipsky (2010) and in the large amount of research conducted by his followers up until this day. This research has persuasively shown that encounters between street-level workers and citizens are far from 'straight-forward' (Lipsky 2010: xi). The complexities of welfare issues are, in other words, no less complex just because they are dealt with in a procedural and rule-abiding type of organisation.

Often, the situation of a citizen is too complex to be reduced to program-matic formats, which is why welfare staff – who ideally must adhere to the rules of the bureaucratic organisation when resolving the problems of citizens – develop discretionary practices rooted in their prior experiences with the particular type of problem. Consequently, welfare workers make discretionary judgements based on the procedures and rules of their work organisation, combined with stereotypical perceptions of the problems of the citizen. The discussions in Chapter 5 show how the rules and principles of the bureaucracy create a key paradox for welfare workers: their work is typically scripted to obtain certain policy objectives even when the work demands that they simultaneously improvise and are sensitive to the individual case or situation. In Lipsky's (2010: xvii) own terms, welfare staff must treat all citizens with similar claims alike (policy as written), but they must also respond to the case of the individual citizen (policy as performed). What is demanded of welfare workers is then to be impartial and rule abiding on the one hand and compassionate and flexible on the other (Lipsky 2010: 15–16), as shown in the case of Mary. This ambiguity will sometimes lead to conflicts between the welfare worker and the citizen (and among welfare staff), because the encountering parties will not always agree on when to follow rules and when to be flexible. This places the welfare staff in a very unique position, because they are the ones who get to decide whether the client is truthful, credible and competent and thereby worthy of their flexibility and potential bypassing of the bureaucratic rules.

Even though there is no doubt that the bureaucratic context is key to analyses of encounters between welfare workers and citizens in present-day welfare organisations, there is a widespread scholarly acknowledgement that not only the bureau-professional regime and administrative discretion affect the welfare encounter (Clarke *et al.* 1994: 22–23). Maynard-Moody and Musheno (2000) suggest viewing discretionary practices as (also) stemming from a different kind of judgement: a judgement of the individual citizen's situation based on the welfare worker's perception of the citizen as either worthy or unworthy of the help offered to them. Their study shows that welfare work in bureaucratic contexts is a much more normatively grounded practice than what Lipsky and many scholars of the so-called street-level bureaucracies have found. According to Maynard-Moody and Musheno (2000), welfare workers are powerful because of their dual positions as both state agents (which gives them formal power as doctors, social workers, judges, etc.) and citizen agents (which gives them the power to define what is best for the citizen).

The latter role of citizen agent is particularly important, because this role – and the consequent authority of welfare workers to interpret the situations of citizens as they see fit – points to the necessity of investigating the norms of welfare encounters. These norms create certain interpretations and 'obvious' ways of categorising the problems of citizens (Mik-Meyer and Villadsen 2014; Gubrium and Järvinen 2014a). However, as suggested by Dubois (2010: 3), a person is neither an impersonal bureaucrat nor a standardised client. Welfare encounters are accordingly inhabited by participants who simultaneously have individual personalities and who play the part of the stereotypical bureaucrat or client. For Dubois, successful encounters in bureaucratic organisations therefore depend on the person's ability to negotiate the stereotypical perceptions of what it means to be a client or a bureaucrat, and in the latter case to apply discretion in this negotiation (Dubois 2010: 4).

When addressing the market context of present-day welfare work, the aim of the book has been to draw attention to the techniques of NPM, such as efficiency, standards and benchmarks, as well as market values, such as service and courtesy, and business values, such as competition, choice, flexibility and respect for the entrepreneurial spirit. There are, in other words, a great number of factors stemming from a market context which affect the encounter between welfare workers and citizens as well. These factors are often labelled as neoliberal (e.g., Broadbent *et al.* 1997; Rogowski 2010), thereby emphasising especially the positioning of the citizen as someone who is capable of choosing and taking responsibility for his or her own life. Within this literature, Western countries are portrayed as having changed from welfare societies to active societies, in which citizens may only gain access to social rights if they are willing to take charge of their own lives and be(come) responsible, active citizens (e.g., Dwyer 2004: 268). This constitutes a form of 4-D dispositional power, which makes certain ways of being in the world valid by empowering them while deeming other (deviant) types of agency as in need of reform. Additionally, today's welfare workers' primary tasks may therefore be neither to deal with bureaucratic principles nor to compensate for the ambiguities within their work through discretionary practices. Their primary task may instead be to act as business and service entrepreneurs with 'can do' attitudes (McCafferty 2010), sales personnel or other roles associated with the market context.

However, values such as competition, choice, flexibility and respect for the entrepreneurial spirit may not be easily integrated into public welfare work (DeLeon and Denhardt 2000: 91; McCafferty 2010). In a market context, citizens are transformed into customers or consumers who are assumed to be in pursuit of their own particular interests. This assumption may cause problems for staff, because citizens' responses and reactions to the various welfare reforms may come across as neither policy-rational – which ideally is the dominant type of rationality employed by welfare workers – nor economic-rational, as expected in a market context of service providers and consumers. In other words, (welfare) customer services assume a particular type of agent whose thinking is based in an economic, legal or policy-rational way of reasoning, which may be a gross oversimplification of both the context in which welfare work takes place and how people think about their situation and their work (Fountain 2001: 66).

The concept of citizen-consumers (Clarke *et al.* 2007) highlights this dilemma, as this hyphenated identity consists of two identifications, which are not usually combined. To be a citizen is a political construct in which, for instance, equality before the law is paramount. However, to be a consumer is an economic construct in which the individual is understood from a market rationale as someone who is engaged in economic transactions and is capable of selectively choosing among different programmes, services and so forth (Clarke *et al.* 2007: 2). Thus, to be identified (and to identify oneself) as a client, patient, citizen or consumer – or as a professional, facilitator or salesperson – brings about complex identity work, because each identification automatically leads to different expectations, such as passive (client), in need of help (patient), equal (citizen) or capable of making economically advantageous choices (consumer).

However, the citizen-consumer identification may also empower citizens because they – by viewing themselves as consumers – may become liberated from the traditional paternalistic power of the welfare state. This identification may ensure a more power-balanced encounter with staff in welfare organisations. However, this type of reasoning assumes that citizens are actually able to challenge the welfare workers and to position themselves as responsible individuals, that is, as someone who is able to make the right choices (as evaluated by the welfare worker) (Clarke *et al.* 2007: 24). In any case, the positioning of citizens as consumers or customers raises the question of whether all citizens are able to take on these demanding roles or if certain individuals or groups of citizens are unable to do so, for instance, individuals who lack the educational resources or the abilities to make relevant choices as seen from the perspective of the (middle-class) welfare workers and their particular norms and ideas. This goal of emphasising the activeness of citizens today also creates new demands of welfare workers, who then must acquire new skills, such as brokering, negotiating and conflict resolution, if they wish to be able to deal with the active citizen (Denhardt and Denhardt 2003: 9). The market context thus seems to create a clash between lay knowledge and expertise, a confrontation between situated and experienced knowledge and the so-called objective (expert) knowledge of professionals (Clarke *et al.* 2007: 115).

There is no doubt that the market context is currently quite powerful, as judged by the number of recent empirical studies which have documented (and often criticised) this approach to the citizen. The reason why this agenda has been accepted in welfare work (or at least to some extent) has to do with two possible factors: firstly, if citizens are active in solving their problems and act in accordance with the expectations and economic or policy rationales of the welfare workers, then this will automatically lead to a quicker (and thus cheaper) way of resolving the problems of citizens. Secondly, the emphasis on citizens to take responsibility and be proactive is likely rooted in a wish to render the (much criticised) patronising welfare state a thing of the past (alongside its authoritarian and condescending staff).

There are many similarities between the contexts of the market and of psychology when discussing the role of citizens and welfare workers today. As in the market, a dominant rationality of the psychological context is the assumption that citizens are responsive individuals who can and ought to voice their situation and make the appropriate choices to improve their lives. However, the expectations of welfare workers differ, as this context expects them to take on roles such as personal advisers, empathic and compassionate mentors, coaches, facilitators and counsellors. This particular framing of the encounter points to a tendency towards individualising and privatising the (social) problems of citizens (Leadbetter and Lownsbrough 2005): social problems are then translated into individualised problems, which can be coached or facilitated by welfare workers. Some scholars therefore suggest that Western societies are presently dealing with a soft type of paternalism (and soft power), which is reflected in descriptions of the welfare state as nurturing and babysitting its citizens (Pykett 2012: 231).

On a more positive note (at least in principle), the norms from psychology and the positioning of the welfare workers as empathic mentors, facilitators and coaches mean that the professional expertise of the welfare workers must give way to the informal knowledge of the citizens, as well as their (possibly opposing) perceptions of their problems and the causes thereof. Within co-production, empowerment and personalisation approaches, the knowledge and engagement of citizens is of paramount importance. However, this allocation of expertise challenges the hitherto privileged status of welfare workers and has (unsurprisingly) resulted in the welfare workers taking a somewhat ambiguous position towards these approaches. The reason for this ambiguity towards centring the citizen and his or her opinions is that it can be difficult to relinquish control for the sole purpose of meeting the demands of emphasising person-centred qualities within welfare work (Needham 2011a).

As the discussions of the book (and present chapter) have revealed, these market- and psychological-inspired approaches to the citizen have received much criticism. Firstly, some scholars argue that these approaches, which place the citizens and their opinions at the absolute centre of the welfare work, are a cover-up for pulling back the welfare state (Durose and Richardson 2016: 36). For instance, in many policy areas the problems of citizens are complex, 'wicked' and 'squishy' (Durose and Richardson 2016:

49), which is why they cannot be resolved by the responsibilisation of the citizen alone, but must involve government as well as professionals and their expertise (and responsibility). Secondly, the reallocation of expertise from the welfare workers to citizens can be regarded as an expression of soft power, as this shift creates an even more ambiguous framing of the encounter than the bureau-professional policy rationale does. Thirdly, the influence of market thinking and norms from psychology leads to an individualisation of social problems, which – rather than being viewed as, in fact, social problems – are then perceived through an individualistic lens and sought to be resolved accordingly.

Powerful welfare encounters

As stated in the preface, my own previous research has greatly centred around how investigations of welfare encounters benefit from combining 2-D, 3-D and 4-D power approaches in the analysis (Hall's [1997] concept of larger environment). For this reason, cases from two of my own research projects have been provided. The first case sought to illustrate how a bureaucratic context, with its emphasis on procedures and the law, affects welfare encounters with citizens who claim to be ill despite lacking biomedical diagnoses. In this particular case, the bureaucratic setup – with municipally employed medical consultants – had strong effects on the perceived legitimacy of the illness of a citizen (as identified by his or her GP). Even though the legitimacy of a citizen's illness claims was based on his or her medical history, the nature and prevalence of the symptoms, the credibility of the patient and the overall evaluation of the symptoms were largely determined by the place of work of the two respective doctors (medical clinic versus municipality), a battle between the fields of medicine and bureaucracy. The case furthermore pointed to the important fact that citizens in Denmark choose their own doctors; thus, if a citizen is unhappy with the work of (or collaboration with) his or her current doctor, then he or she may freely choose a different one. This emphasis on the free choice of citizens in Denmark (which applies not only to health but also to education and other welfare areas) can be seen as ensured by values of the market. However, and as noticed by both caseworkers and the municipal medical consultants, this may bring about unidentifiable biases to a case.

This case further showed how medical descriptions were based on powerful norm-based contexts: certain diagnoses (such as stress) did not grant the citizen the 'patient label' and led instead to a lower (spousal-dependent) financial support, whereas other diagnoses (such as depression) identified the citizen as legitimately ill and provided him or her with the highest possible financial support (independently of spousal income). Finally, the case revealed other contexts as powerful – such as the ICD10 test and the home pages of the Psychiatry Foundation and the Association for Depression – as these diagnostic tools and websites all inform the ways in which the doctors, medical consultants, caseworkers and citizens legitimise and evaluate symptoms or conditions which lack biomedical documentation.

The second case exemplified how a detailed analysis of an encounter between staff and a client in a rehabilitation centre reveals the dominant rationales at play. In this case, the evaluation of a client (Mary) and her resources, as well as norms of emphasising the client's perspective (originating outside the particular situated and observed activity), led to an encounter in which Mary's experiences, the organisation of the welfare work (e.g., formality versus informality) and the procedures of early retirement in her residential municipality took centre-stage. All three factors turned out to greatly affect the evaluation of this particular client's abilities and resources.

This case furthermore revealed how the – after some negotiation – joint description of Mary as a responsive, willing and motivated person (key values within both the market and psychology contexts) united the encountering parties, who ended up working together to ensure her retirement. The analysis thus indicated the inaccuracy of assuming that clients (such as Mary) are unaware that their actions and attitudes affect their possibilities, and not least the evaluations which greatly impact their legal and financial situations. The analysis showed that clients such as Mary – who demonstrate plenty of will and motivation while presumably having few abilities to work – will most likely be regarded by the welfare staff as legitimately ill, despite their lack of biomedical documentation. The analysis demonstrated how bureaucratic principles – which align with the request for biomedical documentation – give way for a psychological approach to her, which affects whether or not the staff considers her a motivated, positive and cooperating client. The analysis pinpointed how norms from psychology – personalisation strategies; strategies of co-production; coaching relationships with clients; empathic, compassionate and informal contact between clients and staff; and so on – had a great impact on the welfare encounter, a soft and seemingly gentle approach of welfare workers. However, the case also suggests that not all clients will succeed in making welfare workers take on their views of their (problem) situation, as it requires certain skills and abilities to be perceived as weak and troubled (as in the case with Mary) that welfare workers will accept the troubles of a citizen as credible and legitimate.

Finally, the two cases demonstrated the importance of applying a relational approach to welfare encounters that brings the agency of both welfare workers and clients to the forefront. This is particularly important because much research tends to overlook the fact that even 'weak' clients (such as Mary) can be powerful participants in welfare encounters, especially if one examines whose definition of the situation, in the end, becomes the winning one. It is thus of utmost importance to emphasise the various norm-based contexts and the skills and abilities to affect the welfare encounter in a specific way if one wishes to understand what goes on in welfare work today. The powerful individuals in present-day welfare encounters may be the staff and citizens who – in line with Dreyfus and Dreyfus' (2005: 780) definition of expertise – are able to make 'immediate intuitive situational responses' which make sense in the situations in which they are part. In other words, the interaction between citizens and welfare workers can only be fully understood through an analytical approach that pays equal attention to structure and agency and hence combines the debates of *power-over* and *power-to*, of domination and empowerment (Haugaard 2012).

References

Abbott, A. (1988). *The System of Professions: An Essay on the Division of Expert Labor*. Chicago: University of Chicago Press.

Abbott, A. (2001). *Chaos of Disciplines*. Chicago: University of Chicago Press.

Allen, D. (2001). Narrating nursing jurisdiction: 'Atrocity stories' and 'boundary-work'. *Symbolic Interaction, 24*(1), 75–103.

Andersen, N. Å. (2007). *Borgerens Kontraktliggørelse*. Copenhagen: Hans Reitzels Publishers.

Atkinson, P. (2014). The reproduction of the professional community. In R. Dingwall and P. Lewis (Eds.), *The Sociology of the Professions: Lawyers, Doctors and Others* (pp. 177–190). New Orleans: Quid Pro Books.

Bachrach, P., and Baratz, M. S. (1962). Two faces of power. *American Political Science Review, 56*(4), 947–952.

Baines, D. (2004). Pro-market, non-market: The dual nature of organizational change in social services delivery. *Critical Social Policy, 24*(1), 5–29.

Baldwin, M. (2000). *Care Management and Community Care: Social Work Discretion and the Construction of Policy*. Aldershot: Ashgate.

Barnes, M. (2011). Abandoning care? A critical perspective on personalisation from an ethic of care. *Ethics & Social Welfare, 5*(2), 153–167.

Bartels, K. P. R. (2013). Public encounters: The history and future of face-to-face contact between public professionals and citizens. *Public Administration, 91*(2), 469–483.

Becker, H. S. (1997). *Outsiders: Studies in the Sociology of Deviance*. London: Free Press.

Bjerge, B., Nielsen, B., and Frank, V. A. (2014). Rationalities of choice and practices of care: Substitution treatment in Denmark. *Contemporary Drug Problems, 41*(1), 57–90.

Bondi, L. (2005). Working the spaces of neoliberal subjectivity: Psychotherapeutic technologies, professionalisation and counselling. *Antipode, 37*(3), 497–514.

Bonoli, G. (2005). The politics of the new social policies: Providing coverage against new social risks in mature welfare states. *Policy & Politics, 33*(3), 431–449.

Bonoli, G. and Natali, D. (2012). The politics of the 'new' welfare states: analysing reforms in Western Europe. In G. Bonoli and D. Natali (Eds.), *The Politics of the New Welfare States* (pp. 3–20). Oxford: Oxford University Press.

Bourdieu, P. (1991). *Language and Symbolic Power: The Economy of Linguistic Exchanges*. Cambridge: Polity Press.

Bourdieu, P. (1998). *Practical Reason: On the Theory of Action*. Stanford: Stanford University Press.

Bourdieu, P. (2000). *Outline of a Theory of Practice*. Cambridge: Cambridge University Press.

Bourdieu, P. (2011). The forms of capital. In I. Szeman and T. Kaposy (Eds.), *Cultural Theory: An Anthology* (pp. 81–93). Singapore: Blackwell-Wiley.

Bourdieu, P., and Wacquant, L. (1996). *An Invitation to Reflexive Sociology*. Cambridge: Polity Press.

Bovaird, T. (2007). Beyond engagement and participation: User and community coproduction of public services. *Public Administration Review, 67*(5), 846–860.

Brandon, T. (2005). Classic review. *Disability & Society, 20*(7), 779–783.

Brehm, J., and Gates, S. (1997). *Working, Shirking, and Sabotage: Bureaucratic Response to a Democratic Public*. Ann Arbor: University of Michigan Press.

Brint, S. (1994). *In an Age of Experts: The Changing Role of Professionals in Politics and Public Life*. Princeton: Princeton University Press.

Broadbent, J., Dietrich, M., and Roberts, J. (1997). The end of the professions? In J. Broadbent, M. Dietrich, and J. Roberts (Eds.), *The End of the Professions? The Restructuring of Professional Work* (pp. 1–13). London: Routledge.

Bröckling, U. (2015). *The Entreprenereual Self: Fabricating a New Type of Subject*. London: Sage Publications.

Brodkin, E. Z. (2011). Policy work: Street-level organizations under new managerialism. *Journal of Public Administration Research and Theory, 21*(Supplement 2), i253–i277.

Brugnoli, A., and Colombo, A. (2012). Introduction. In A. Brugnoli and A. Colombo (Eds.), *Government, Governance and Welfare Reform: Structural Changes and Subsidiary in Italy and Britain* (pp. ix–xii). Cheltenham: Edward Elgar Publishing.

Cahn, E. S. (2000). *No More Throw-Away People. The Co-Production Imperative*. Washington: Essential Books.

Carr, E. S. (2010). Enactments of expertise. *Annual Review of Anthropology, 39*(1), 17–32.

Cassell, E. J. (2004). *The Nature of Suffering and the Goals of Medicine*. New York: Oxford University Press.

Chandler, D. (2000). Active citizens and the therapeutic state: The role of democratic participation in local government reform. *Policy & Politics, 29*(1), 3–14.

Chriss, J. J. (1999). Introduction. In J. J. Chriss (Ed.), *Counseling and the Therapeutic State*. New York: Aldine de Gruyter.

Clarke, A., Cochrane, A., and McLaughlin, E. (1994). *Managing Social Policy*. London: Sage Publications.

Clarke, J. (2005). New Labour's citizens: Activated, empowered, responsibilized, abandoned? *Critical Social Policy, 25*(4), 447–463.

Clarke, J., Newman, J., Smith, N., Vidler, E., and Westmarland, L. (2007). *Creating Citizen-Consumers: Changing Publics and Changing Public Services*. London: Sage Publications.

Cowden, S., and Singh, G. (2007). The 'user': Friend, foe or fetish? A critical exploration of user involvement in health and social care. *Critical Social Policy, 27*(1), 5–23.

Cruikshank, B. (1999). *The Will to Empower: Democratic Citizens and Other Subjects*. Ithaca: Cornell University Press.

Cutler, T., Waine, B., and Brehony, K. (2007). A new epoch of individualization? Problems with the 'personalization' of public sector services. *Public Administration, 85*(3), 847–855.

Dahl, R. A. (1957). The concept of power. *Behavioral Science, 2*(3), 201–215.

Davis, K. (1988). *Power under the Microscope*. Dordrecht: Foris Publications.

Dean, H. (2003). The Third Way and social welfare: The myth of post-emotionalism. *Social Policy & Administration, 37*(7), 695–708.

DeLeon, L., and Denhardt, R. B. (2000). The political theory of reinvention. *Public Administration Review, 60*(2), 89–97.

Denhardt, R. B., and Denhardt, J. V. (2000). The new public service: Serving rather than steering. *Public Administration Review, 60*(6), 549–559.

Denhardt, R. B., and Denhardt, J. V. (2003). The new public service: An approach to reform. *International Review of Public, 8*(1), 3–10.

Dingwall, R. (2014/1983). Introduction. In R. Dingwall and P. Lewis (Eds.), *The Sociology of the Professions: Lawyers, Doctors and Others* (pp. 1–12). New Orleans: Quid Pro Books.

Dingwall, R., and Lewis, P. (Eds.). (2014). *The Sociology of the Professions: Lawyers, Doctors and Others*. New Orleans: Quid Pro Books.

Dobson, R. (2015). Power, agency, relationality and welfare practice. *Journal of Social Policy, 44*(4), 687–705.

Dreher, J. (2016). The social construction of power: Reflections beyond Berger/Luckmann and Bourdieu. *Cultural Sociology, 10*(1), 53–68.

Dreyfus, H. L., and Dreyfus, S. E. (2005). Peripheral vision: Expertise in real world contexts. *Organization Studies, 26*(5), 779–792.

du Gay, P. (2000). *In Praise of Bureaucracy*. London: Sage.

Dubois, V. (2010). *The Bureaucrat and the Poor: Encounters in French Welfare Offices*. Surrey: Ashgate.

Durkheim, E. (1982). *The Rules of Sociological Methods*. New York: Free Press.

Durose, C., and Richardson, L. (2016). *Designing Public Policy for Co-production: Theory, Practice and Change*. Bristol: Policy Press.

Duyvendak, J. W., Knijn, T., and Kremer, M. (2006). Policy, people and the new professional: An introduction. In J. W. Duyvendak, T. Knijn, and M. Kremer (Eds.), *Policy, People and the New Professional: De-Professionalisation and Re-Professionalisation in Care and Welfare*. (pp. 7–16). Amsterdam: Amsterdam University Press.

Duyvendak, J. W., Knijn, T., and Kremer, M. (Eds.). (2006). *Policy, People, and the New Professional: De-Professionalisation and Re-Professionalisation in Care and Welfare*. Amsterdam: Amsterdam University Press.

Dworkin, R. (1978). *Taking Rights Seriously*. London: Duckworth.

Dwyer, P. (2004). Creeping conditionality in the UK: From welfare rights to conditional entitlements? *Canadian Journal of Sociology, 29*(2), 265–287.

Ecclestone, K., and Brunila, K. (2015). Governing emotionally vulnerable subjects and 'therapisation' of social justice. *Pedagogy, Culture & Society, 23*(4), 485–506.

Ellis, K. (2011). 'Street-level bureaucracy' revisited: The changing face of frontline discretion in adult social care in England. *Social Policy & Administration, 45*(3), 221–244.

Emirbayer, M., and Johnson, V. (2008). Bourdieu and organizational analysis. *Theory and Society, 37*, 1–44.

Emirbayer, M., and Williams, E. M. (2005). Bourdieu and social work. *Social Service Review, 79*(4), 689–724.

Ernst, R., Nguyen, L., and Taylor, K. C. (2013). Citizen control: Race at the welfare office. *Social Science Quarterly, 94*(5), 1283–1307.

Evans, T. (2011). Professionals, managers and discretion: Critiquing street-level bureaucracy. *British Journal of Social Work, 41*(2), 368–386.

Evans, T., and Harris, J. (2004). Street-level bureaucracy, social work and the (exaggerated) death of discretion. *British Journal of Social Work, 34*(6), 871–895.

Evers, A., and Guillemard, A.-M. (2013). Introduction: Marchall's concept of citizenship and contemporary reconfiguration. In A. Evers and A.-M. Guillemard (Eds.), *Social Policy and Citizenship: The Changing Landscape* (pp. 3–34). New York: Oxford University Press.

Evetts, J. (2003). The sociological analysis of professionalism: Occupational change in the modern world. *International Sociology, 18*(2), 395–415.

Evetts, J. (2006). Short note: The sociology of professional groups: New directions. *Current Sociology, 54*(1), 133–143.

Evetts, J. (2009a). New professionalism and New Public Management: Changes, continuities and consequences. *Comparative Sociology, 8*(2), 247–266.

Evetts, J. (2009b). The management of professionalism. A contemporary paradox. In S. Gewirtz, P. Mahony, I. Hextall, and A. Cribb (Eds.), *Changing Teacher Professionalism: International Trends, Challenges and Ways Forward* (pp. 19–30). Abingdon: Routledge.

Evetts, J. (2011). A new professionalism? Challenges and opportunities. *Current Sociology, 59*(4), 406–422.

Eyal, G. (2013). For a sociology of expertise: The social origins of the autism epidemic. *American Journal of Sociology, 118*(4), 863–907.

Fan, Y. (2008). Soft power: Power of attraction or confusion? *Place Branding & Public Diplomacy, 4*(2), 147–158.

Ferguson, H. (2001). Social work, individualization and life politics. *British Journal of Social Work, 31*(1), 41–55.

Ferguson, I. (2007). Increasing user choice or privatizing risk? The antinomies of personalization. *British Journal of Social Work, 37*(3), 387–403.

Fotaki, M. (2011). Towards developing new partnerships in public services: Users as consumers, citizens and/or co-producers in health and social care in England and Sweden. *Public Administration, 89*(3), 933–955.

Foucault, M. (1983). The subject and power. In H. L. Dreyfus and P. Rabinow (Eds.), *Michel Foucault, Beyond Structuralism and Hermeneutics* (pp. 208–226). New York: Harvester Wheatsheaf.

Foucault, M. (1987). *Mental Illness and Psychology*. Berkeley: University of California Press.

Fountain, J. E. (2001). Paradoxes of public sector customer service. *Governance: An International Journal of Policy and Administration*, 14(1), 55–73.

Freidson, E. (2004). *Professionalism: The Third Logic*. Cambridge: Polity Press.

Freidson, E. (2014). The theory of professions: State of the art. In R. Dingwall and P. Lewis (Eds.), *The Sociology of the Professions: Lawyers, Doctors and Others* (pp. 13–28). New Orleans: Quid Pro Books.

Friedli, L., and Stearn, R. (2015). Positive affect as coercive strategy: Conditionality, activation and the role of psychology in UK government workfare programmes. *Medical Humanities*, 41(1), 40–47.

Giddens, A. (1984). *The Constitution of Society*. Cambridge: Polity Press.

Goffman, E. (1967). *Interaction Ritual: Essays on Face-to-Face Behavior*. Garden City: Doubleday.

Goffman, E. (1970). *Strategic Interaction*. Oxford: Basil Blackwell.

Goffman, E. (1974). *Asylums: Essay on the Social Situation of Mental Patients and Other Inmates*. Harmondsworth: Penguin Books.

Goffman, E. (1981). *Forms of Talk*. Philadelphia: Philadelphia University Press.

Goffman, E. (1983). The interaction order: American Sociological Association, 1982 presidential address. *American Sociological Review*, 48(1), 1–17.

Goffman, E. (1990a). *Stigma: Notes on the Management of Spoiled Identity*. Harmondsworth: Penguin.

Goffman, E. (1990b). *The Presentation of Self in Everyday Life*. New York: Doubleday.

Goss, S. (2001). *Making Local Governance Work: Networks, Relationships and the Management of Change*. Basingstoke: Palgrave Macmillan.

Greener, I. (2002). Agency, social theory and social policy. *Critical Social Policy*, 22(4), 688–705.

Grover, C. (2009). Privatizing employment services in Britain. *Critical Social Policy*, 29(3), 487–509.

Gubrium, J. F. (1986). *Oldtimers and Alzheimer's: The Descriptive Organization of Senility*. Greenwich: JAI Press.

Gubrium, J. F., and Holstein, J. A. (Eds.). (2001). *Institutional Selves: Troubled Identities in a Postmodern World*. New York: Oxford University Press.

Gubrium, J. F., and Järvinen, M. (Eds.). (2014a). *Turning Troubles into Problems. Clientization in Human Service*. London: Routledge.

Gubrium, J. F., and Järvinen, M. (2014b). Troubles, problems, and clientization. In J. F. Gubrium and M. Järvinen (Eds.), *Turning Troubles into Problems: Clientization in Human Services* (pp. 1–13). London: Routledge.

Habermas, J. (1984). *The Theory of Communicative Action: Reason and the Rationalisation of Society*. Boston: Beacon Press.

Hacking, I. (1999). *The Social Construction of What?* Cambridge, MA: Harvard University Press.

Hall, C., Slembrouck, S., Haigh, E., and Lee, A. (2010). The management of professional roles during boundary work in child welfare. *International Journal of Social Welfare*, *19*(3), 348–357.

Hall, P. M. (1997). Meta-power, social organization and the shaping of social action. *Symbolic Interaction*, *20*(4), 397–418.

Hall, R. H. (1963). The concept of bureaucracy: An empirical assessment. *American Journal of Sociology*, *69*(1), 32–40.

Hallett, T. (2003). Symbolic power and organizational culture. *Sociological Theory*, *21*(2), 128–149.

Hallett, T. (2007). Between deference and distinction: Interaction ritual through symbolic power in an educational institution. *Social Psychology Quarterly*, *70*(2), 148–171.

Harrits, G. S., and Møller, M. Ø. (2014). Prevention at the front line: How home nurses, pedagogues, and teachers transform public worry into decisions on special efforts. *Public Management Review*, *16*(4), 447–480.

Haugaard, M. (1997). *The Construction of Power: A Theoretical Analysis of Power, Knowledge and Structure*. Manchester: Manchester University Press.

Haugaard, M. (2003). Reflections of seven ways of creating power. *European Journal of Social Theory*, *6*(1), 87–113.

Haugaard, M. (2012). Rethinking the four dimensions of power. *Journal of Political Power*, *5*(1), 35–54.

Haydock, W. (2014). The rise and fall of the 'nudge' of minimum unit pricing: The continuity of neoliberalism in alcohol policy in England. *Critical Social Policy*, *34*(2), 260–279.

Hayward, C., and Lukes, S. (2008). Nobody to shoot? Power, structure, and agency: A dialogue. *Journal of Power*, *1*(1), 5–20.

Hochschild, A. R. (1983). *The Managed Heart: Commercialization of Human Feeling*. Berkeley: University of California Press.

Hodge, S. (2005). Participation, discourse and power: A case study in service user involvement. *Critical Social Policy*, *25*(2), 164–179.

Hoggett, P. (2001). Agency, rationality and social policy. *Journal of Social Policy*, *30*(1), 37–56.

Holstein, J. A., and Gubrium, J. F. (2000). *The Self We Live By: Narrative Identity in a Postmodern World*. New York: Oxford University Press.

Hood, C. (1991). A public management for all seasons? *Public Administration*, *69*, 3–19.

Horwath, J. (2000). Childcare with gloves on: Protecting children and young people in residential care. *British Journal of Social Work*, *30*(2), 179–191.

Huising, R. (2015). To hive or to hold? Producing professional authority through scut work. *Administrative Science Quarterly*, *60*(2), 263–299.

Hunter, S. (2003). A critical analysis of approaches to the concept of social identity in social policy. *Critical Social Policy*, *23*(3), 322–344.

Hunter, S. (2012). Ordering differentiation: Reconfiguring governance as relational politics. *Journal of Psycho-Social Studies*, *6*(1), 3–29.

Hupe, P., and Hill, M. (2007). Street-level bureaucracy and public accountability. *Public Administration, 85*(2), 279–299.

Isin, E. F. (2004). The neurotic citizen. *Citizenship Studies, 8*(3), 217–235.

Järvinen, M., and Mik-Meyer, N. (Eds.). (2003). *At Skabe en Klient – Institutionelle Identiteter i Socialt Arbejde*. Copenhagen: Hans Reitzels Publishers.

Järvinen, M., and Mik-Meyer, N. (Eds.). (2012). *At Skabe en Professionel*. Copenhagen: Hans Reitzels Publishers.

Jenkins, R. (2008). Erving Goffman: A major theorist of power? *Journal of Power, 1*, 157–168.

Jenkins, R. (2013). The ways and means of power: Efficacy and resources. In S. R. Clegg and M. Haugaard (Eds.), *The SAGE Handbook of Power* (pp. 140–156). London: Sage Publications.

Jenson, J. (2012). A new politics for the social investment perspective: objectives, instruments, and areas of intervention in welfare regimes. In G. Bonoli and D. Natali (Eds.) *The politics of the new Welfare states* (pp. 21–44). Oxford: Oxford University Press.

Jones, C. (2001). Voices from the front line: State social workers and New Labour. *British Journal of Social Work, 31*(4), 547–562.

Jones, R., Pykett, J., and Whitehead, M. (2010). Governing temptation: Changing behaviour in an age of libertarian paternalism. *Progress in Human Geography, 35*(4), 483–501.

Jones, R., Pykett, J., and Whitehead, M. (2013). *Changing Behaviours: On the Rise of the Psychological State*. Cheltenham: Edward Elgar Publishing.

Jos, P. H., and Tompkins, M. E. (2009). Keeping it public: Defending public service values in a customer service age. *Public Administration Review, 69*(6), 1077–1086.

Jutel, A. (2010). Medically unexplained symptoms and the disease label. *Social Theory & Health, 8*(3), 229–245.

Kuhlmann, E., Allsop, J., and Saks, M. (2009). Professional governance and public control: A comparison of healthcare in the United Kingdom and Germany. *Current Sociology, 57*(4), 511–528.

Leadbetter, D., and Lownsbrough, H. (2005). *Personalisation and Participation: The Future of Social Care in Scotland*. London: Demos.

Lessenich, S. (2011). Constructing the socialized self: Mobilization and control in the active society. In U. Bröckling, S. Krasmann, and T. Lemke (Eds.), *Governmentality: Current Issues and Future Challenges* (pp. 304–320). London: Routledge.

Lewis, J., and Glennerster, H. (1996). *Implementing the New Community Care*. Buckingham: Open University Press.

Liljegren, A. (2012). Pragmatic professionalism: Micro-level discourse in social work. *European Journal of Social Work, 15*(3), 295–312.

Lipsky, M. (2010/1980). *Street-Level Bureaucracy: Dilemmas of the Individual in Public Services*. New York: Russell Sage Foundation.

Lister, R. (2001). Towards a citizens' welfare state: The 3 + 2 'R's of welfare reform. *Theory, Culture & Society, 18*(2–3), 91–111.

Lloyd, L. (2010). The individual in social care: The ethics of care and the 'person-alisation agenda' in services for older people in England. *Ethics & Social Welfare*, 4(2), 188–200.

Loseke, D. R. (1989). Creating clients: Social problems work in a shelter for battered women. In J. A. Holstein and G. Miller (Eds.), *Perspectives on Social Problems* (1st ed.). Greenwich: JAI Press.

Loseke, D. R. (1992). *The Battered Woman and Shelters: The Social Construction of Wife Abuse*. Albany: State University of New York Press.

Loseke, D. R. (1999). *Thinking about Social Problems: An Introduction to Constructionist Perspectives*. New York: Aldine de Gruyter.

Loseke, D. R. (2001). Lived realities and formula stories of 'battered women'. In J. F. Gubrium and J. A. Holstein (Eds.), *Institutional Selves: Troubled Identities in a Postmodern World* (pp. 107–126). New York: Oxford University Press.

Lucio, J. (2009). Customers, citizens, and residents: The semantics of public service recipients. *Administration & Society*, 41(7), 878–899.

Ludwig-Mayerhofer, W., Behrend, O., and Sondermann, A. (2014). Activation, public employment services and their clients: The role of social class in a continental welfare state. *Social Policy & Administration*, 48(5), 594–612.

Lukes, S. (2005). *Power: A Radical View* (2nd ed.). Basingstoke: Palgrave Macmillan.

Lymbery, M. E. F. (2003). Negotiating the contradictions between competence and creativity. *Journal of Social Work*, 3(1), 99–117.

Manning, P. (2000). Credibility, agency, and the interaction order. *Symbolic Interaction*, 23(3), 283–297.

Maynard-Moody, S., and Musheno, M. (2000). State agent or citizen agent: Two narratives of discretion. *Journal of Public Administration Research and Theory*, 10(2), 329–358.

Maynard-Moody, S., and Musheno, M. (2003). *Cops, Teachers, Counsellors: Stories from the Front Lines of Public Service*. Ann Arbor: University of Michigan Press.

Maynard-Moody, S., and Musheno, M. (2012). Social equities and inequities in practice: Street-level workers as agents and pragmatists. *Public Administration Review*, 72(Special Issue 1), 16–23.

Mayo, M. (2013). Providing access to justice in disadvantaged communities: Commitments to welfare revisited in neo-liberal times. *Critical Social Policy*, 33(4), 679–699.

McBeath, G., and Webb, S. A. (2002). Virtue ethics and social work: Being lucky, realistic, and not doing ones duty. *British Journal of Social Work*, 32, 1015–1036.

McCafferty, P. (2010). Forging a 'neoliberal pedagogy': The 'enterprising education' agenda in schools. *Critical Social Policy*, 30(4), 541–563.

McDonald, C., and Marston, G. (2005). Workfare as welfare: Governing unemployment in the advanced liberal state. *Critical Social Policy*, 25(3), 374–401.

McDonald, C., Marston, G., and Buckley, A. (2003). Risk technology in Australia: The role of the job seeker classification instrument in employment services. *Critical Social Policy*, 23(4), 498–525.

Mik-Meyer, N. (1999). *Kærlighed og Opdragelse i Socialaktiveringen*. Copenhagen: Gyldendal Publishers.

Mik-Meyer, N. (2004). *Dømt til Personlig Udvikling: Identitetsarbejde i Revalidering*. Copenhagen: Hans Reitzels Publishers.

Mik-Meyer, N. (2007). Interpersonal relations or jokes of social structure? Laughter in social work. *Qualitative Social Work*, 6(1), 9–26.

Mik-Meyer, N. (2009). Identities and organisations: Evaluating the personality traits of clients in two Danish rehabilitation organizations. *Critical Practice Studies*, 8(1), 32–48.

Mik-Meyer, N. (2010a). An illness of one's own: Power and the negotiation of identity among social workers, doctors, and patients without a bio-medical diagnosis. *Journal of Power*, 3(2), 171–187.

Mik-Meyer, N. (2010b). Putting the right face on a wrong body: An initial interpretation of fat identities in social work organizations. *Qualitative Social Work*, 9(3), 385–405.

Mik-Meyer, N. (2011). On being credibly ill: Class and gender in illness stories among welfare officers and clients with medically unexplained symptoms. *Health Sociology Review*, 20(1), 28–40.

Mik-Meyer, N. (2014). The imagined psychology of being overweight in a weight loss program. In J. F. Gubrium and M. Järvinen (Eds.), *Turning Troubles into Problems: Clientization in Human Services* (pp. 102–118). London: Routledge.

Mik-Meyer, N. (2015a). Gender and disability: Feminising male employees with visible impairments in Danish work organisations. *Gender, Work & Organization*, 22(6), 579–595.

Mik-Meyer, N. (2015b). Health in a risk perspective: The case of overweight. In T. T. Bengtsson, M. Frederiksen, and J. E. Larsen (Eds.), *The Danish Welfare State: A Sociological Investigation* (pp. 139–152). New York: Palgrave Macmillan.

Mik-Meyer, N. (2016a). Disability and 'care': Managers, employees and colleagues with impairments negotiating the social order of disability. *Work, Employment & Society*, 30(6).

Mik-Meyer, N. (2016b). Disability, sameness, and equality: Able-bodied managers and employees discussing diversity in a Scandinavian context. *Scandinavian Journal of Disability Research*.

Mik-Meyer, N. (2016c). Othering, ableism and disability: A discursive analysis of co-workers' construction of colleagues with visible impairments. *Human Relations*, 69(6), 1341–1363.

Mik-Meyer, N., and Johansen, M. B. (2009). *Magtfulde Diagnoser og Diffuse Lidelser*. Frederiksberg: Samfundslitteratur.

Mik-Meyer, N., and Obling, A. R. (2012). The negotiation of the sick role: General practitioners' classification of patients with medically unexplained symptoms. *Sociology of Health and Illness*, 34(7), 1025–1038.

Mik-Meyer, N., and Villadsen, K. (2014). *Power and Welfare: Understanding Citizens' Encounters with State Welfare*. New York: Routledge.

Miller, G. (1992). Human service practice as social problems work. In G. Miller (Ed.), *Current Research on Occupations* (pp. 3–22). Greenwich: JAI Press.

Miller, G. (2001). Changing the subject: Self-construction in brief therapy. In J. F. Gubrium and J. A. Holstein (Eds.), *Institutional Selves: Troubled Identities in a Postmodern World* (pp. 64–83). New York: Oxford University Press.

Mladenov, T., Owens, J., and Cribb, A. (2015). Personalisation in disability services and healthcare: A critical comparative analysis. *Critical Social Policy*, *35*(3), 307–326.

Moore, D. (2009). 'Workers', 'clients' and the struggle over needs: Understanding encounters between service providers and injecting drug users in an Australian city. *Social Science and Medicine*, *68*(6), 1161–1168.

Needham, C. (2008). Realising the potential of co-production: Negotiating improvements in public services. *Social Policy and Society*, *7*(2), 221–231.

Needham, C. (2011a). *Personalising Public Services: Understanding the Personalisation Narrative*. Bristol: Policy Press.

Needham, C. (2011b). Personalization: From story-line to practice. *Social Policy & Administration*, *45*(1), 54–68.

Needham, C., and Glasby, J. (Eds.). (2014). *Debates in Personalisation*. Bristol: Policy Press.

Needham, C., and Glasby, J. (2015). Personalisation – Love it or hate it? *Journal of Integrated Care*, *23*(5), 268–276.

Newman, J., Barnes, M., Sullivan, H., and Knops, A. (2004). Public participation and collaborative governance. *Journal of Social Policy*, *33*(2), 203–223.

Newman, J., and Tonkens, E. (2011a). Introduction. In J. Newman and E. Tonkens (Eds.), *Participation, Responsibility and Choice: Summoning the Active Citizen in Western European Welfare States* (pp. 9–28). Amsterdam: Amsterdam University Press.

Newman, J., and Tonkens, E. (2011b). Active citizenship: Responsibility, choice and participation. In J. Newman and E. Tonkens (Eds.), *Participation, Responsibility and Choice: Summoning the Active Citizen in Western European Welfare States* (pp. 179–202). Amsterdam: Amsterdam University Press.

Nolan, J. (1998). *The Therapeutic State: Justifying Government at Century's End*. New York: New York University Press.

Noordegraaf, M. (2007). From 'pure' to 'hybrid' professionalism: Present-day professionalism in ambiguous public domains. *Administration & Society*, *39*(6), 761–785.

Nye, J. S. (1990). Soft power. *Foreign Policy 80*, 153–172.

Nye, J. S. (2011). Power and foreign policy. *Journal of Political Power*, *4*(1), 9–24.

OECD (Organisation for Economic Co-operation and Development). (1997). Beyond 2000: The New Social Policy Agenda. Conference summary. Paris: OECD.

Osborne, D. and Gaebler, T. (1992). *Reinventing Government: How the Entrepreneurial Spirit is Transforming the Public Sector*. New York: Addison-Wesley Publication.

Peters, B. G., and Pierre, J. (2000). Citizens versus the new public manager: The problem of mutual empowerment. *Administration & Society*, *32*(1), 9–28.

Polsky, A. J. (1991). *The Rise of the Therapeutic State*. Princeton: Princeton University Press.

Prior, D., and Barnes, M. (2011). Subverting social policy on the front line: Agencies of resistance in the delivery of services. *Social Policy & Administration*, *45*(3), 264–279.

Pykett, J. (2009). Personalization and de-schooling: Uncommon trajectories in contemporary education policy. *Critical Social Policy*, *29*(3), 374–397.

Pykett, J. (2010). Citizenship education and narratives of pedagogy. *Citizenship Studies*, 14(6), 621–635.

Pykett, J. (2012). The new maternal state: The gendered politics of governing through behaviour change. *Antipode*, 44(1), 217–238.

Pykett, J., Saward, M., and Schaefer, A. (2010). Framing the good citizen. *British Journal of Politics and International Relations*, 12(4), 523–538.

Renedo, A., and Marston, C. (2014). Spaces for citizen involvement in healthcare: An ethnographic study. *Sociology*, 49(3), 488–504.

Richardson, L., Purdam, K., Cotterill, S., Rees, J., Squires, G., and Askew, R. (2014). Responsible citizens and accountable service providers? Renegotiating the contract between citizen and state. *Environment and Planning A*, 46, 1716–1731.

Rogowski, S. (2010). *Social Work: The Rise and Fall of a Profession?* Bristol: Policy Press.

Rose, N. (1998). *Inventing Our Selves: Psychology, Power, and Personhood*. Cambridge: Cambridge University Press.

Rose, N. (1999). *Powers of Freedom: Reframing Political Thought*. Cambridge: Cambridge University Press.

Rose, N. (2000). Community, citizenship, and the Third Way. *American Behavioral Scientist*, 43(9), 1395–1411.

Rose, N., and Miller, P. (2010). Political power beyond the state: Problematics of government. *British Journal of Sociology*, 61(Supplement 1), 271–303.

Rosenthal, P., and Peccei, R. (2006). The social construction of clients by service agents in reformed welfare administration. *Human Relations*, 59(12), 1633–1658.

Rueschemeyer, D. (2014). Professional autonomy and the social control of expertise. In R. Dingwall and P. Lewis (Eds.), *The Sociology of the Professions: Lawyers, Doctors and Others* (pp. 29–44). New Orleans: Quid Pro Books.

Ryan, K. (2007). *Social Exclusion and the Politics of Order*. Manchester: Manchester University Press.

Schinkel, W., and Noordegraaf, M. (2011a). Professionalism as symbolic capital: Materials for a Bourdieusian theory of professionalism. *Comparative Sociology*, 10(1), 67–96.

Schinkel, W., and Noordegraaf, M. (2011b). Professional capital contested: A Bourdieusian analysis of conflicts between professionals and managers. *Comparative Sociology*, 10(1), 97–125.

Sciulli, D. (2005). Continental sociology of professions today: Conceptual contributions. *Current Sociology*, 53(6), 915–942.

Scourfield, P. (2007). Social care and the modern citizen: Client, consumer, service user, manager and entrepreneur. *British Journal of Social Work*, 37(1), 107–122.

Sementelli, A. (2006). Government is them: How traveling the road to Wellville can undermine the legitimacy of public administration. *International Journal of Organization Theory and Behaviour*, 9(1), 92–116.

Singh, P. (2015). Pedagogic governance: Theorising with/after Bernstein. *British Journal of Sociology of Education*, 1–20.

Spector, M., and Kitsuse, J. I. (2001). *Constructing Social Problems*. New Brunswick: Transaction Publishers.

Speed, E., and Gabe, J. (2013). The Health and Social Care Act for England 2012: The extension of 'new professionalism'. *Critical Social Policy*, *33*(3), 564–574.

Spicker, P. (2006). *Policy Analysis for Practice*. Bristol: Policy Press.

Spicker, P. (2013). Personalisation falls short. *British Journal of Social Work*, *43*(7), 1259–1275.

Stenner, P., Barnes, M., and Taylor, D. (2008). Editorial introduction. Psychosocial welfare: Contributions to an emerging field. *Critical Social Policy*, *28*(4), 411–414.

Stokes, T., Dixon-Woods, M., and Williams, S. (2006). Breaking the ceremonial order: Patients' and doctors' accounts of removal from a general practitioner's list. *Sociology of Health and Illness*, *28*(5), 611–636.

Taylor-Gooby, P. (1999). Markets and motives: Trust and egoism in welfare markets, *Journal of Social Policy*, *28*(1), 97–114.

Taylor-Gooby, P. (2004). Open markets and welfare values: Welfare values, inequality and social change in the silver age of the welfare state. *European Societies*, *6*(1), 29–48.

Taylor-Gooby, P. (2010). *Reframing Social Citizenship*. Oxford: Oxford University Press.

Thévenot, L. (2011). Power and oppression from the perspective of the sociology of engagements: A comparison with Bourdieu's and Dewey's critical approaches to practical activities. *Irish Journal of Sociology*, *19*(1), 35–67.

Torstendahl, R. (2005). The need for a definition of 'profession'. *Current Sociology*, *53*(6), 947–951.

Valverde, M. (1998). *Diseases of the Will: Alcohol and the Dilemmas of Freedom*. Cambridge: Cambridge University Press.

Wacquant, L. (2013). Symbolic power and group-making: On Bourdieu's reframing of class. *Journal of Classical Sociology*, *13*(2), 274–291.

Wagenaar, H. (2004). 'Knowing' the rules: Administrative work as practice. *Public Administration Review*, *64*(6), 643–655.

Weber, M. (2013). *Economy and Society: An Outline of Interpretive Sociology* (Vol. 2). Berkeley: University of California Press.

Whitaker, G. (1980). Co-production: Citizen participation in service delivery. *Public Administration Review*, *40*, 240–246.

Wilensky, H. L. (1964). The professionalization of everyone? *American Journal of Sociology*, *70*(2), 137–158.

Wright, S. (2012). Welfare-to-work, agency and personal responsibility. *Journal of Social Policy*, *41*(2), 309–328.

Index

EU authorised representative for GPSR:
Easy Access System Europe, Mustamäe tee 50,
10621 Tallinn, Estonia
gpsr.requests@easproject.com